Internment in
Britain in 1940

D1627954

Ines Newman has worked in local government policy. She has published several articles on local economic development and one sole authored book: I. Newman, 2014, *Reclaiming Local Democracy: A progressive future for local government* (Bristol: Policy Press). She has spent the last three years researching family history.

Charmian Brinson, Emeritus Professor of German, Imperial College London. Her research interests focus in particular on the study of German and Austrian exiles in Britain between 1933 and 1945. She has published extensively in this area including: C. Brinson, A. Müller-Härlin, J. Winckler, 2009, *'His Majesty's Loyal Internee': Fred Uhlman in Captivity* (London: Vallentine Mitchell).

Rachel Dickson (MA, Courtauld Institute) Head of Curatorial Services, Ben Uri Gallery and Museum, has published widely on exiled artists, most recently on art in internment for: M. Bohm-Duchen (ed.), 2019, *Insiders Outsiders: Refugees from Nazi Europe and their Contribution to British Visual Culture* (London: Lund Humphries).

Internment in Britain in 1940

Life and Art Behind the Wire

Ines Newman

with Charmian Brinson and Rachel Dickson

VALLENTINE MITCHELL

LONDON • CHICAGO, IL

First published in 2021 by Vallentine Mitchell

Catalyst House,	814 N. Franklin Street,
720 Centennial Court,	Chicago, Illinois,
Centennial Park, Elstree WD6 3SY, UK	IL 60610 USA

www.vmbooks.com

Copyright © 2021 Ines Newman, Charmian Brinson and Rachel Dickson

British Library Cataloguing in Publication Data:
An entry can be found on request

ISBN 978 1 912676 47 7 (Paper)
ISBN 978 1 912676 48 4 (Cloth)
ISBN 978 1 912676 49 1 (Ebook)

Library of Congress Cataloging in Publication Data:
An entry can be found on request

Contents

Preface and Acknowledgements

My much-loved brother, Ralph Oppenheimer, had always been interested in family history. Sometime after Google appeared he found that the Wiener Library in London had a diary written by our grandfather, Wilhelm Hollitscher. He was a financial supporter of the Library. We had not known about the diary and we still do not know who gave it to the Wiener Library. My family had arrived in England in the spring of 1949, over five years after my grandfather had died. My mother must have known about the diary as her father told her about it in his letters and left it to her in his will but there is no evidence she ever looked at it. He wrote to her in Egypt at least once a week so maybe she felt that she knew the material contained in the diary or she didn't know it had been given to the Library. Our mother died in 1954 and although we saw her brother when he visited the UK from the west coast of America, we knew very little about our grandparents.

Ralph encouraged our interest in the diary. I first went to the library in 2013 to meet the archivist, Howard Falksohn, and look at the manuscript. It was in fourteen exercise books written in neat, but to us illegible, German handwriting. Katy Jackson of the Wiener Library found Noemi Zell who is the first key person I want to thank for helping us with this book. She managed to transcribe sections so my eldest sister, Hannah Edmonds, could translate it. Hannah was a French and German teacher and German is her first language. I'm not sure she really wanted to work as a translator and I'm aware I nagged her into this job as my German is non-existent. From the age of about 4-5, when my father used to amuse German guests by asking me to say '*Spaetzle*', I have always refused to speak German. *Spaetzle* are a German egg noodle dumpling which my father loved, being a Swabian German from Stuttgart. I hated them!

Hannah is really the co-author of this book. She has done all the translations and, in the chapter on Wilhelm, I have used some of her description of him. Translating the diary proved fun, with Hannah dictating while I typed it up. It was an enjoyable sister co-production. I am very grateful that she accepted my nagging and helped me on this project. Ralph's death on 1 April 2016 spurred us on with the realisation that our time was limited and unless we completed this task our children and grandchildren would not have access to important parts of their family history.

As we worked through the diary, we got to his description of his internment in Huyton and how he sat for his portrait painted by Hugo Dachinger. So I set out on a quest to find the portrait. I started in August 2017 by writing and sending a copy of a photo of my grandfather to the National Museums Liverpool, Walker Art Gallery which had mounted an exhibition *Art Behind Barbed Wire* in 2004. Here I was to meet the next person who was central to this book. Alex Patterson is a curator at the Museum and her assistance has been invaluable. She originally replied to my query by saying that the five male portraits in the Walker Art Gallery collection did not look like my grandfather but suggested I contact the Manx museum and independent art dealers who had previously dealt with or sold Dachinger's work. I asked for further advice on how to find these art dealers and was surprised to receive an email a week later on 14 August 2017 from Alex, with an image attached saying she had been looking at the Blouin Art Sales Index, a database they use to value works of art. She continued: 'Interestingly my attention was caught by the first item on the list entitled "Portrait of a man, head and shoulders". I think the gentleman in the picture looks remarkably like your grandfather. What do you think?'

I agreed the image did look like him. It was lovely to get my first view of the portrait, albeit in a thumbnail picture. I immediately wrote to Roseberys Fine Art London who had sold the painting on 28 June 2016. Several nagging emails and phone calls later, I finally got the brush off at the end of October 2017 when a cataloguer at Roseberys replied: 'Unfortunately client confidentiality, with regard to who bought the painting from us, means we are unable to contact them with your details, as most purchasers do not want to be contacted by third parties, even if it is from a harmless research point of view.'

I could not think where to go next. On 15 March 2018 I had been pruning the roses and when I stepped down off our ladder, I slipped and fell back on the stone steps. I had injured a rib on my back and was sitting on the sofa watching News at Ten on the BBC and feeling very sorry for myself. When the local news came on there was on item on the Ben Uri Gallery exhibition *Out of Austria: Austrian artists in exile in Great Britain, 1933-1945*. Suddenly Dachinger's portrait of my grandfather appeared on the screen and I leapt out of the sofa in excitement, despite my pain. Had Alex not sent me the small image I wouldn't have recognised the portrait so quickly and may not have known that it was my grandfather.

I immediately wrote to Sarah MacDougall (who is the Head of Collections and BURU [Ben Uri Research Unit for the Study of the Jewish and Immigrant Contribution to the Visual Arts in Britain since 1900] Ben Uri Gallery and Museum) and she responded very positively. Soon Hannah and I went to meet Sarah and her co-curator, Rachel Dickson, at the Gallery. These two are the next people I need to thank. The Ben Uri Gallery is lucky to have two such knowledgeable and engaging curators. They have been more than helpful, organising high-quality reproductions of the painting for all the extended family and always ready to help beyond the call of duty.

Rachel put in a proposal for a talk on our grandfather's portrait at the very prestigious *Understanding British Portraits* seminar on 9 October 2018 at the National Portrait Gallery. The portrait was chosen and I went along with my sisters. The talk was brilliant: well-illustrated and researched with excellent delivery. While Rachel was researching it, we went through our grandfather's letters to my mother and found many more references to Hugo Dachinger. My grandfather saw him regularly after Huyton. The plan to publish the diary at that stage is discussed in Rachel's chapter in this book. Wilhelm was clearly very excited about this proposal and disappointed when it came to nothing. It has therefore been fantastic to realise his dream and to publish the diary now with the Dachinger paintings as he originally proposed.

I want to thank Vallentine Mitchell for accepting my book proposal and making this all possible. The decision to go ahead rested with Toby Harris; Lisa Hyde has been the editor of the book; and Jenni Tinson has been in charge of production advising on the images of the pictures. They have all been helpful and supportive but particular thanks go to Lisa who gave me useful advice about editing the diary and who has had a significant input into the book.

I would not have wanted to publish the diary without the context being explained. So my very sincere thanks go to both Rachel Dickson and Charmian Brinson for agreeing to write their chapters.I think they provide a significant contribution and in addition are of high quality and very readable. I hope the readers of this book agree.

We needed the co-operation of both the Ben Uri Gallery and the Walker Gallery Liverpool to publish all the paintings in this book. They were both very generous. Alex Patterson and her colleague Jessie showed us the whole collection of 38 Dachinger paintings that they hold and our daughter Hannah helped me select the most appropriate ones for the book. It was a privilege to see them all and the Gallery is looking after them with care.

Nathan Pendlebury, the Image Reproduction Administrator at National Museums Liverpool, then supplied high resolution images for the ones we chose. Dachinger's daughter-in-law, Anne Dachinger and his daughter, Miriam Murphy, enthusiastically gave us copyright permission to reproduce the paintings in the book for which we are very grateful. Louise Weller of Pallant House facilitated contact with Walter Nessler's son, Conrad Marshall-Purves, who also kindly gave permission to use one of Nessler's sketches of the camp in the book. We hope this book will widen the knowledge of the talent that came to the UK from Nazi Germany and appreciation of Dachinger and his fellow artists.

We would also like to thank several people who have helped by supplying images or information about images, including: Peter Biller at the University of York; Yvonne Cresswell and Jude Dicken at Manx National Heritage; Frances Elliott and Sue Holdich for the Estate of Charles Rosner; Justin Piperger, photographer (portrait of Hollitscher and images from Ben Uri Collection); Julie Seldon for the Estate of Alfred Lomnitz and Louise Weller at Pallant House Gallery; and Claudia Suppan from Suppan Fine Arts, Vienna. David Glasser, Chairman, Ben Uri Gallery and Museum, has been supportive of this project throughout the process.

Lin Rice, the Community History Librarian at the Archive Resources for Knowsley (ARK), has been very helpful, searching through the archive to see if she can find out more about the many internees my grandfather mentions in the diary. Jennifer Taylor from the Research Centre for German and Austrian Exile Studies, IMLR, University of London facilitated all of us in accessing her excellent edited book with eye-witness accounts of internment in Huyton which was published by the Anglo-German Family History Society. My nephew David Edmonds, author of '*The Murder of Professor Schlick: The Rise and Fall of the Vienna Circle*', provided invaluable help in resolving many of the puzzles about passages in Wilhelm's diary that I could not understand.

Charmian would also like to thank The National Archives, Kew; Deutsches Exilarchiv, Deutsche Nationalbibliothek, Frankfurt a.M.; Österreichische Nationalbibliothek, Vienna; and Lambeth Palace Library.

Finally my personal thanks go to my husband, Mike, who is the real academic writer in the family and helped me with footnotes and commented on drafts. He is my partner in everything.

Ines Newman
April 2020

List of Illustrations

Front cover: Hugo Dachinger, *Portrait of Wilhelm Hollitscher*, 1940, watercolour and gouache on newsprint, Ben Uri Collection © Artist's Estate, photo: courtesy of Ben Uri Gallery and Museum.

1. *Paul Hamann's Drawing Class*, Hugo Dachinger, 1962. Ben Uri Collection © The Estate of Hugo Dachinger, photo: courtesy of Ben Uri Gallery and Museum.
2. *Bell Street Market*, Hugo Dachinger, 1977. Ben Uri Collection © The Estate of Hugo Dachinger, photo: courtesy of Ben Uri Gallery and Museum.
3. Photo of Hugo and Meta Dachinger and their daughter Miriam © Dachinger Estate, courtesy Suppan Fine Arts, Vienna.
4. The Tent, Huyton. Walter Nessler, 1940. The Walker, National Museums Liverpool. © Artist's Estate.
5. *Jooss: 20 Jahre für den Tanz* (Jooss: 20 Years of Dance) Hugo Dachinger and Fritz Rosen, Huyton 1940. The Walker, National Museums Liverpool. © Artist's Estate.
6. *Line of Internees Following a Soldier with Rifle*. Hugo Dachinger, Huyton 1940. The Walker, National Museums Liverpool. © Artist's Estate.
7. Photo of Charles Rosner (Károly Rosner, 1902-1972) reproduced with permission from Frankie Elliott (known also as artist Frankie Partridge).
8. Front cover of *Never Mind, Mr. Lom* by Alfred Lomnitz (London, Macmillan & Co Ltd, 1941), reproduced with permission of the Lansdale family.
9. Wilhelm Hollitscher, 1/10/1933, black and white photograph, © Oppenheimer family.
10. Simon Hollitscher with his granddaughter Lisl, at a holiday house in Austria. The photo was taken by Lisl's brother Hansl when he was around 16 in 1927 © Oppenheimer family.

Colour Plates

Plate 3: *Portrait of a Man in Blue Sweater and Brown Jacket, His Right Hand Raised to his Head*, Hugo Dachinger, 1940, watercolour and gouache on wallpaper, National Museums Liverpool, Walker Art Gallery, © The Estate of Hugo Dachinger, Photograph courtesy of National Museums Liverpool.

Plate 4: *Two Internees Bowing in Front of an Officer*, Hugo Dachinger, 1940, pen, ink and watercolour on paper, National Museums Liverpool, Walker Art Gallery, © The Estate of Hugo Dachinger, Photograph courtesy of National Museums Liverpool.

Plate 5: *Portrait of a Man Wearing Blue Shirt and Red Tie*, Hugo Dachinger, 1940, gouache on newspaper, National Museums Liverpool, Walker Art Gallery, © The Estate of Hugo Dachinger, Photograph courtesy of National Museums Liverpool.

Plate 6: *Dinner in Campton Park: Vitamins Enlisted to Win the War*, Hugo Dachinger, 1940, watercolour and gouache on newspaper, National Museums Liverpool, Walker Art Gallery, © The Estate of Hugo Dachinger, Photograph courtesy of National Museums Liverpool.

Plate 7: *Identity Lost*, Hugo Dachinger, 1940, pastel, watercolour and gouache on newspaper, National Museums Liverpool, Walker Art Gallery, © The Estate of Hugo Dachinger, Photograph courtesy of National Museums Liverpool.

Plate 8A: *Dead End*, Hugo Dachinger, 1940, watercolour and gouache on newspaper and canvas, National Museums Liverpool, Walker Art Gallery, © The Estate of Hugo Dachinger, Photograph courtesy of National Museums Liverpool.

Plate 8B: *Perimeter Fence Under Red Sky*, Hugo Dachinger, 1940, watercolour and gouache on newspaper, National Museums Liverpool, Walker Art Gallery, © The Estate of Hugo Dachinger, Photograph courtesy of National Museums Liverpool.

Back cover: Hugo Dachinger, *Art Behind Barbed Wire* poster for Redfern Gallery exhibition. Image courtesy of Manx National Heritage (2002-0103).

1

The Internment of Aliens in Britain during the Second World War: A Tale of Panic and Confusion

Charmian Brinson

When war broke out in September 1939, there were up to 80,000 German-speakers – men and women principally from Germany, Austria and Czechoslovakia – seeking refuge in Britain.[1] Hitler's rise to power in Germany early in 1933, followed soon after by the Reichstag Fire, had led to the persecution of groups opposed to National Socialism: socialists, communists, liberals, intellectuals and others. Many were arrested and held in the newly-established concentration camps such as Dachau, near Munich. Racial persecution followed hard on the heels of political persecution, with the Jews forming a particular target, especially after the passing of the Nuremberg Laws in 1935 that sought to exclude Jewish citizens from German society and civil rights. As early as 1933, the emigration from Germany of far-sighted anti-Nazis and of Jews (not mutually exclusive groups, of course) had already begun, to any countries that would accept them. France, Czechoslovakia and the other countries bordering on Germany were particularly sought-after destinations in the early days when the reluctant refugees still expected the Hitler regime to fall and the restoration of normal life to follow. Other refugees, however, were already setting their sights further afield, on Palestine, Britain and the USA, although entry into these countries was by no means straightforward. In Britain, although visas were not introduced until 1938, and despite a financial guarantee for Jewish refugees from the leaders of the Anglo-Jewish community, new arrivals were frequently granted only a short time stay, together with a condition prohibiting most forms of employment. German-Jewish immigration into Palestine was limited by the British Mandate-holders' desire not to stir up Arab hostility and, consequently, by the introduction of a quota system. The USA, too, operated a quota system which might involve applicants in a wait of several years.

In the meantime, the German exodus, which continued to grow, was soon joined by similar waves of migration from Austria and Czechoslovakia, following the *Anschluss*, i.e. the annexation of Austria by the Germans in March 1938, and the German invasions of the Sudetenland in October 1938 and of rump Czechoslovakia in March 1939. The terrifying events of the 'Crystal Night' (*Kristallnacht*) pogrom of November 1938, when Jews were attacked, arrested and humiliated, Jewish properties were destroyed, and synagogues torched, served as a deadly serious warning to those who were still hesitant about leaving.

With the onset of war, Germans and Austrians in Britain, both men and women, were declared 'enemy aliens' and called to appear in front of Aliens' Tribunals throughout Britain. The purpose of the tribunals was to grade refugees and other Germans and Austrians resident in Britain in accordance with their perceived level of risk to the British cause: those categorized 'A', for example, were deemed a security risk and interned immediately. This categorization was applied to 569 German-speaking aliens (in addition to an earlier group of 415 on the MI5 Security List who had been arrested and imprisoned at or even before the start of the war).[2] 6,782 category 'B' refugees, about whom it was thought that some doubt could be held to exist, were subject to certain restrictions; while 64,244 category 'C's, the great majority of the refugee population, were deemed loyal to the British cause and remained unrestricted.[3] Although the whole procedure was generally well intentioned, it was also permeated through and through by inconsistency and confusion. Not infrequently, the decisions reached were influenced by the prejudice or indeed ignorance of the British tribunal chairmen, who often had little understanding of the German situation. There was particular inconsistency when it came to the doubtful 'B' cases: certain tribunals automatically categorized all domestic servants as 'B', for example. As for the apparently dangerous category 'A' cases, while there were doubtless genuine threats to British security among them, it was reported that there were probably as many anti-Nazis and Jews categorized as 'A' as there were actual Nazis. At Olympia, for instance, where some of the early category 'A' prisoners were held, Bernhard Weiss, the Jewish ex-Vice President of Berlin, upon whose head the Nazis had put a price of 20,000 marks, rubbed shoulders with Ernst Hanfstängl, Hitler's former friend and piano player.[4]

Unlike in the First World War, it was not the original intention of the British authorities to introduce a policy of mass alien internment, not least because of the large numbers of refugees among the alien population; indeed the Home Secretary, Sir John Anderson, specifically ruled this out at the start of the war. All this had changed, however, by mid-1940 because of the deteriorating war situation: over the first few months of 1940, the German army invaded and occupied one country after another. Denmark, Norway, Holland, Belgium and France, in turn, fell to the Germans, with the fall of France, in particular, being a cause of acute anxiety for its British ally. Indeed, by June 1940, with German forces ranged along the French coast, the invasion of Britain looked like a very real threat. The general British nervousness was exacerbated by rumours of fifth column activity by German 'refugees' in the newly occupied countries, as expressed for instance in a memorandum by Sir Nevile Bland (former British Minister to the Hague), drawing on his recent experiences in Holland:

> I have not the least doubt that, when the signal is given […] there will be satellites of the monster all over the country who will at once embark on widespread sabotage and attacks on civilians and the military indiscriminately. We cannot afford to take the risk. *All* Germans and Austrians at least ought to be interned at once.[5]

Certain sections of the British press, such as the *Daily Mail* and *Daily Express* and other likeminded newspapers, began to clamour for the internment of the 'enemy aliens' in their midst. In the *Daily Mail*, for example, which throughout the 1930s had shown itself sympathetic to the rise of fascism, their foreign correspondent G. Ward Price maintained:

> All refugees from Austria, Germany and Czechoslovakia, men and women alike, should be drafted without delay to a remote part of the country and kept under strict supervision […] As the head of a Balkan State said to me last month: 'In Britain you fail to realise that *every* German is an agent.'[6]

As a mood close to hysteria began to take hold among sections of the general British public, as well as among some parliamentarians, and their view was backed up by the perennially suspicious security services, the pressure on the government increased and the Home Office bowed to the panic. Consequently, on 16 May 1940, the category 'B' men were interned followed by, on 27 May, the category 'B' women. From 10 June it was the turn of the Italians, many of whom had been resident in Britain for years. Italy had entered the war on the Axis side that same day, providing the impetus that led Winston Churchill to issue his frequently cited instruction: 'Collar the Lot!' Finally, from 22 June, the category 'C' German and Austrian men, constituting by far the largest group, and including the author of the diary reproduced in this book, Wilhelm Hollitscher, were rounded up. With very few exceptions, Category 'C' women were never interned which explains why male internees so far outnumbered their female equivalents. In all, approximately 25,000 men and 4,000 women were interned, mostly though not exclusively German-speaking refugees.[7]

Hollitscher's arrest on 26 June and subsequent internment ran along lines typical at that time: police arrived at his door early in the morning, allowed him an hour to pack, took him to the local police station and from there to a larger holding area, in his case Chelsea Barracks, where he found himself one of a hundred category 'C' 'enemy aliens'. From there they were transported to a transit camp, Kempton Park, the collecting station for the London region, where the numbers swelled to 1,800 and confusion reigned. Kempton was one of several racecourses used as an emergency measure and conditions were primitive, with next to no furniture and inadequate food and medical facilities. Other transit camps, 'tent camps', such as the one at Prees Heath, were entirely or almost entirely under canvas, and arguably enjoyed even worse conditions than the racecourse camps. One of the most unusual of the transit camps was that situated at Ascot in the winter quarters of Bertram Mills's circus where previously the circus animals had been kept. But undoubtedly the worst was the camp at Warth Mills, a derelict vermin-ridden cotton mill near Bury, where the lavatory provision for 2,000 men consisted of 60 buckets in the yard and the washing facilities of 18 water taps and 1 bathtub. Worse than that, the British soldiers – and even their officers – helped themselves in plain sight to the inmates' possessions.[8]

Considerable resentment was caused a little later in the internment process when internees discovered that others had managed to avoid police arrest by the simple expedient of leaving home early in the morning, usually before 6 a.m., and absenting themselves from the house for some hours – evidently the police were unlikely to call again later in the day. Anecdotal evidence has it that the mornings could be pleasantly spent in Hyde Park or in Lyons Corner House until it was safe to return home. Both Martin Miller, the actor renowned for his satirical portrayal of Adolf Hitler, and Erich Fried, the young poet of later fame, are said to have escaped internment in this way. Hollitscher's heart condition was not considered sufficient grounds for exemption from internment, though others were luckier, especially those with good contacts. Georg Knepler, for instance, the musician who played the leading role in the cultural activities of the Austrian Centre – a large-scale refugee organization based in London – was evidently exempted on account of his wife's serious operation at that time.[9] Other leading members of refugee bodies, such as the Communist Heinz Schmidt of the Free German League of Culture, were exempted because of their organisational roles in the refugee community (much to the disapproval of MI5, which would have preferred to see Communists interned).[10]

From the transit camps, the internees were transported to more permanent camps, a number of which were situated on the Isle of Man (where aliens had previously been held during the First World War). Here, they were billeted in the hotels designed for the tourist trade. Though still behind barbed wire, and subject to the initial confusion that characterized the whole British internment process, the internees were provided with rather less spartan accommodation than they had suffered in the primitive transit camps.

Wilhelm Hollitscher, however, was not among those sent to the Isle of Man but rather to Huyton Camp, near Liverpool, a newly-built but unfinished council estate. It had been founded in May 1940, in time for the first group of category 'B' internees, and held upwards of 3,000 men – sometimes as many as 5,000 – at any one time. The reason for the fluctuating population was that Huyton, too, was conceived as a transit camp so that batches of internees were periodically transferred into and out of the camp. In his diary, Hollitscher records the departure of numerous fellow internees for the Isle of Man or the Dominions (see below), including his portraitist Hugo Dachinger to Mooragh Camp, Isle of Man; and it is likely that Hollitscher, too, would have been transferred to the Isle of Man had he not been released after just over two months' internment.

Less has been written about life in Huyton Camp than in the better-known Isle of Man internment camps such as Hutchinson and Onchan.[11] However, although unlike the latter camps, Huyton produced no camp newspaper that would have recorded aspects of everyday life, there are – apart from Hollitscher's own diary – several extant accounts from fellow Huytonians. These include one covering much the same period of time as Hollitscher's, and therefore supplementing it rather fruitfully, from the elderly pacifist Otto Lehmann-Russbueldt (although one should bear in mind that Hollitscher's document is personal and Lehmann-Russbueldt's official in character).[12] In the camp's unfinished state, there was initially no furniture, no soap or toilet paper, no hot water, no proper medical facilities and insufficient food. Straw-filled palliasses functioned as beds. The unfinished houses provided basic accommodation, with twelve or more internees per house, but the overspill, particularly the under-25s, were relegated to tents. Perhaps worse than that, Lehmann-Russbueldt, whose internment journey from Kempton to Huyton and whose age and poor state of health mirrored Hollitscher's, recorded the hostility and suspicion towards the internees displayed by their British guards – and some of the British misapprehensions. One officer had later explained to an interned German professor that he had initially believed that the internees were all secret Nazis. Another had expressed his surprise that there were so many Jews among the Nazis. Yet another had believed that the internees were all prisoners of war.[13] It should be noted, however, that Hollitscher's experience was not quite the same: he mentions the 'more peaceful reception' he encountered at Huyton as compared with that at Kempton Park.

As in the other male internment camps – the women's internment experience was somewhat different[14] – the organisation of day-to-day camp life was largely a matter for the internees themselves. There was an internee hierarchy made up of democratically elected house fathers, street fathers and a camp father who together took necessary decisions, passed down instructions and represented the internees with the British camp authorities. The camp father was the distinguished Austrian physicist, Professor Karl Weissenberg, previously from the University of Berlin, who in emigration had been working at Southampton University. Hollitscher's house father was another well-known figure from within the German-speaking emigration, the German trade unionist and Social Democrat Hans Gottfurcht.

A feature of all the Second World War internment camps in Britain, to a greater or lesser degree, was the self-organisation of cultural, educational and intellectual life, and Huyton was no exception. Interned in Huyton, there were artists, academics and professional men of all kinds – it is said that there were at least 22 university professors there, for example[15] – leading to all manner of lectures, classes, musical events and the art exhibition that Hollitscher describes in his diary. There was even, from early August 1940, an Old Vienna Café that served as an attractive social meeting place. Through this rich cultural mix, Hollitscher came into contact with men who, like Gottfurcht, were celebrated figures within different sections of the German refugee community. One of these was the Austrian poet, Fritz Gross, well-known in certain refugee circles for the lending library that he ran from his basement flat in Bloomsbury, who reportedly took part in a 'poetic evening', reading works created in the camp. Another was the pedagogue Hans Siebert, lecturing on Goethe – though not at all to

Hollitscher's liking – who was a leading light in both the Free German League of Culture and later the London-based Freie Deutsche Hochschule or Free German Institute.

While the majority of the camp population was Jewish, observant and non-observant, as in the refugee population as a whole, there was also a minority of non-Jewish internees, for instance political refugees like Lehmann-Russbueldt. Most of the internees were Germans or Austrians, but there were others – around 350 of them –who in one way or another had become caught up in the internment process, including Czechs, Poles and even Turks and some self-styled Englishmen who, despite their British parentage, had had the misfortune to be born in Germany. In addition, there was a group of elderly men who, though originally German, had virtually lost the ability to speak German, having been resident in Britain for decades.[16]

The despair many of the internees experienced at being cut off from their families and, at least initially, at being deprived of news of any kind, led to several cases of suicide and to increased tension within the camp. The original Huyton Commandant was reportedly obsessed with security, hence the ban on newspapers and radio and the introduction of other repressive measures, such as the removal of all metal objects from the camp that could conceivably be used in a riot. Lehmann-Russbueldt even reports that a barber, who was in possession of electric shears, had to relinquish them every evening to prevent them from being used as a secret transmitter.[17] Things improved, however, with the appointment of the much more effective Lt. Col. Slatter as Commandant on 15 July who relaxed some of the sterner rulings of his predecessor. Indeed, Hollitscher records that, from that same day, newspapers were permitted in the camp and that he and his housemates had placed an immediate collective order of four papers, the *Manchester Guardian, Daily Telegraph, Sunday Times* and *Picture Post*. Under the previous Commandant, the only papers to which internees had had access were those smuggled in on the black market, an enterprise in which it is thought that the guards played a significant part. Internees wishing to read the illegally obtained newspaper, for a limited time only, had to pay a fee that was calculated on a sliding scale.

The introduction of radio, too, into the camp was due to the liberalising attitude of Lt. Col. Slatter – prior to his arrival, listening to the radio, as with reading the newspaper, was prohibited for internees. Where Hollitscher and his housemates were concerned, it seems probable that the influential Hans Gottfurcht, Hollitscher's house father, who enjoyed good relations with the British Labour Party and Trade Union Movement, served as an additional source of information: on 13 July, we read in Hollitscher's diary, for example, of an exchange of telegrams between Gottfurcht and a British correspondent who was in a position to read out Gottfurcht's telegram to the House of Commons.

A further frustration to being deprived of news, probably a greater one, was the extreme slowness of the internee mail, caused by the fact that the letters both in and out of all the internment camps had to be censored in Liverpool by a staff insufficiently large for the task. Particularly at the beginning, letters piled up in the sorting offices and could take weeks to arrive at their destination. Moreover, the delay did not merely lead to the lack of family news, though this could be upsetting enough; it also affected the internees' correspondence with legal representatives, for example, regarding their applications for release, or with the US and other Embassies regarding vital visa appointments.

In these circumstances, it is interesting to try to gauge how much or how little Hollitscher knew of the events taking place in the outside world. On 7 July, for example, he reported on rumours that men over 60, i.e. those between 60 and the upper limit of 70, would be set free; and on a variation of these rumours, four days later, that release of internees over 65 (of whom Hollitscher was one) was under consideration. Again on 7 July, he noted that three influential British newspapers, *The Times,* the *Daily Telegraph* and the *Manchester Guardian*, had commented on the shameful handling of the refugees. By then, even without regular access to the press, Hollitscher was apparently aware not only that there were Englishmen and women vigorously taking the part of the refugees, but also that there had been a general sea change in public opinion towards them. On 10 July he recorded that the well-known British author H.G. Wells had published a powerful article in the refugees' favour, 'J'accuse', in *Reynold's News;*[18] and on 11 July that the Independent MP for the Combined English Universities, known widely (and in some quarters derisively) as 'The Member for Refugees' because of her tireless advocacy of the refugee cause, had condemned their plight in Parliament. The Eleanor Rathbone speech in question was undoubtedly her contribution to the celebrated six-hour debate on refugees, internment and deportation that took place in the House of Commons on 10 July, which Hollitscher refers to in his diary a few days later, on 13 July. Other parliamentarians taking part on this occasion included Major Victor Cazalet, Colonel Josiah Wedgwood, Graham White and Wilfrid Roberts, all MPs well-known for their support for the German and Austrian refugees from Hitler.[19]

What Hollitscher fails to mention in his diary, however, is the main reason for the British change of heart: the deportation of hundreds of

German, Austrian and Italian internees, together with prisoners of war, to Canada in late June/early July 1940 and the sinking of one of the deportation ships, the *Arandora Star*, on 2 July in mid-Atlantic, with great loss of life. This took place very shortly after Hollitscher had been transferred to Huyton Camp, and the news of the ill-fated ship appears to have escaped him, at that time at any rate. Otto Lehmann-Russbueldt, on the other hand, who reached Huyton on 5 July, reports that rumours concerning the fate of the *Arandora Star* had awaited him there on arrival, even though the reading of newspapers was forbidden.[20]

While Hollitscher does not record this particular event, he does comment, on 6 July, on the question then being hotly debated in camp as to whether internees were prepared to volunteer for transport overseas. He also reports on the confused events of a few days later concerning a list of men designated for deportation which, proving inadequate, had led to the forcible and random deportation of others, regardless of their age and circumstances. Although it was not known at the time, these men were bound for Australia and had a gruelling journey ahead of them on the *Dunera*.

The policy of deportation stemmed from the same fear that had brought about mass internment in the first place: that, in the event of a German invasion, pro-German internees would aid the invaders. Deportation was intended to apply to category 'A' refugees only (in addition to prisoners of war), but it was carried out in such a state of confusion that all categories of refugees were included on the lists. The British Dominions were requested to take over the custody of several thousand internees, designated as dangerous, from Britain, and the Canadian and Australian Governments agreed to assist Britain in its hour of need. Four ships were dispatched to Canada between 21 June and 7 July 1940, the *Arandora Star* being the second of these. Despite the sinking, on 10 July the *Dunera*, the fifth ship, departed for Australia, the passenger list including a number of presumably traumatised survivors from the *Arandora Star*. So inhumane was the treatment of the deportees by the British crew who, among other acts of cruelty, helped themselves to the refugees' possessions and threw their suitcases overboard, that an official enquiry was held the following year, the officers court martialed and the refugees financially recompensed for their loss.

It was, above all, the fate of the *Arandora Star* that brought about the change in the British population who were shocked at the plight of helpless refugees being turned on by British officialdom. Indeed, indiscriminate internment appears to have ceased altogether by around 15 July 1940, though no official announcement was ever made. This meant that those refugees who had evaded police arrest up to this point, as discussed earlier, could escape internment altogether. In his diary, Hollitscher begins to note visits to the camp by various eminent Englishmen and women with a reformist agenda, such as one by the Bishop of Chichester, George Bell, on 18 July. Bell was well known for his passionate support of the refugees and was often criticised for it. In a debate in the House of Lords on 12 July, following on from that in the Commons two days before, he had protested:

> I venture to think – and I have some knowledge in this matter – that internment of aliens of German and Austrian origin, irrespective of character, irrespective of their attitude to the Nazi regime, irrespective of their devotion to the interests and cause of this country and our Allies, is demanded neither by national security nor by justice.[21]

His arguments were sharply countered by the Conservative peer Lord Marchwood who, he said, could only assume that, like himself, 'most of your Lordships must have listened to the Right Reverend Prelate with amazement', for 'one would almost imagine he does not appear to realise that we are at war and that the lives of our own people would be endangered if we were to carry out the suggestions which he makes so glibly'.[22]

George Bell's brief visit to Huyton on 18 July was the first of several visits he would make to the internment camps. Bell took a particular interest in a group of internees whom he had been responsible for bringing to Britain between Christmas 1938 and September 1939. This was a group of 33 'non-Aryan' pastors of the German Confessional Church, that is to say Christian pastors of Jewish descent (for whom the Jewish charitable agencies did not hold themselves specifically responsible). Since their arrival in Britain, they had been largely employed in the few Lutheran parishes in Britain or in Anglican parishes. Bell was dismayed at the internment not only of clergy from this group but also of some of their wives. In addition, Bell chose to make himself responsible for other interned German clergymen such as the resident pastors of the German congregations in Britain. In Huyton, Bell reportedly saw 50 internees, including the Camp Father, Karl Weissenberg, and some of 'his' pastors (though other pastors had already left Huyton for the Isle of Man which Bell would visit subsequently).[23]

As Hollitscher notes, on the same day as Bell's visit, a second leading religious figure visited the camp, namely the British-born rabbi of

Hungarian extraction, Dr Solomon Schonfeld. Schonfeld, like Bell, was an inspirational figure who prior to the war had been responsible for saving thousands of Jews from Austria, including the organisation of a *Kindertransport* of around 300 Orthodox Jewish children. In his capacity as Executive Director of the Chief Rabbi's Religious Emergency Council, Schonfeld visited numerous alien internment camps where he concerned himself particularly with the welfare of the Orthodox internees, such as the provision of kosher food.

Two days after that, on 20 July, the Liberal MP Graham White, a member of the Parliamentary Committee on Refugees, founded by Eleanor Rathbone, and a prominent speaker in the six-hour debate of 10 July, visited Huyton, together with Rathbone herself, as part of a fact-finding Parliamentary Commission. Arguably, however, the most significant of the visits that the great and the good paid to Huyton during the two months Hollischer spent there was that of Lord Lytton, Chairman of the Advisory Council on Aliens, on 11 August. The Advisory Council's remit was to ensure the welfare of internees and Lytton was asked to advise on and rectify many of the outstanding difficulties in the camp. One of the chief complaints, as Hollitscher first notes on 16 July, was the presence of a Nazi group in the camp, led by a Sudeten German from the kitchen staff by the name of 'Gunter'. The mixing of refugee and National Socialist internees, some of the latter having been resident in Britain for years prior to the war, was by no means confined to Huyton but loomed large as a problem in the Isle of Man camps as well. Accommodated in boarding houses there, the internees normally slept in the double beds intended for the holiday trade, which sometimes involved the pairing of a Jewish refugee with a Nazi sleeping partner, especially in the early chaotic days of internment. This was obviously an intolerable situation which was at least partially solved by the fact that the Nazis, who were mostly category 'A' refugees, were selected for deportation (though clearly not all of the Nazis from Huyton were included). The problem was perhaps worst in Rushen, the women's internment camp, where the National Socialist internees were reportedly felt to be a threatening and brooding presence (since the deportation policy was never extended to women).[24]

Other internee problems discussed with Lord Lytton included the lack of air raid shelters, despite the fact that Huyton was situated close to Liverpool which was a target for enemy bombing. It is interesting, though, how acclimatised many of the internees became to air raid sirens and to the raids themselves, with Hollitscher noting on 15 August, for example, that when the siren had sounded during a refugee talent contest, 99 per cent of the audience had remained in their seats. Yet, at the same time, with both press and radio now bringing news into the camp from the outside world, he was well aware of the Battle of Britain raging overhead, of air battles over London, of the planes shot down, of the 'young lives lost' (19 August).

However, there was little that agitated the internee population so much as the delay in their mail, and this too, even after weeks of the internment process and some slight improvement in this area, was discussed with Lytton. Immediately following his visit to Huyton, on 13 August, Lytton put the problem to the Home Secretary, Sir John Anderson, who assured him that as far as the Office of Postal Censorship was concerned, the delay should now not exceed a period of 24 hours; nevertheless, the rerouting of refugee mail through Liverpool might still cause some delay.[25] Other internee complaints that Lytton took directly to Anderson stemmed at least in part from the unfinished nature of the housing estate: food was still being prepared in the open air, for example, there was no laundry and the hospital arrangements were inadequate. Lytton also suggested that modifications could usefully be made to the release process that could well be expedited for certain groups of internees, particularly those British in all but name, and others who had built up businesses in Britain and were employing a British workforce.[26]

Release was, of course, a major topic of conversation, in Huyton as in the other internment camps, and rumour abounded, as mentioned above. Finally, regulations concerning release from internment were published in three governmental White Papers that created a procedure for release[27] (though their implementation took its time, leading to great impatience in the refugee population). The first of these, published on 31 July 1940, set out eighteen different categories of refugee who were eligible, for example: the old, the young, the infirm and also those engaged in work of national importance such as scientists, doctors and workers in industry or agriculture. The second White Paper appeared a month later, at the end of August, and contained a nineteenth category, namely 'any person who by his writing or speeches or political or official activities [...] has consistently, over a period of years, taken a public and prominent part in opposition to the Nazi system and is actively friendly towards the Allied cause'. The third White Paper of October 1940 included the further category of 'persons of eminent distinction who have made outstanding contributions to Art, Science, Learning or Letters'.

Hollitscher had previously made several attempts to obtain his release on the grounds of the heart complaint that troubled him throughout his internment, but he had not been successful. In the end it was not his state of health that brought about his release but rather a ruling that reduced the upper age limit for internment from 70 to 65, clearing the way for the 67 year-old's release on 1 September 1940. But Hollitscher was by no means alone in being medically unfit for internment since Huyton contained an unusually high proportion of sick and elderly men. It was calculated that 40 per cent of the camp population were over 50 and that 33 per cent were suffering from serious complaints such as diabetes, heart trouble, gastric problems, paralysis, blindness and various mental afflictions – illnesses that would have indicated unfitness for internment in a better-regulated system.[28]

All in all, internment in Huyton Camp proved an arduous experience, arguably even more so than in the other longer-term internment camps, a fact that was probably due as much as anything to its provisional nature and constantly shifting population. On 13 July, a member of the Swiss Legation (as neutral 'protecting power') visited the group of interned 'Aryan' Germans on behalf of the German Government and concluded, according to Hollitscher, that he had 'never seen such a miserable camp'. The Austrian writer Robert Neumann's internment journey took him through three internment camps, Cowley, Huyton and finally Mooragh on the Isle of Man; he wrote in his diary of 'the hell of Huyton' and the 'unprecedented chaos' he experienced there, and volunteered at the first possible opportunity for transfer to the Isle of Man.[29] Wilhelm Hollitscher's reactions to Huyton were rather more sanguine, however: despite ill health, he refers to his internment as an 'adventure', valuing the chance it gave him to meet 'some fantastic people'. Yet from time to time he still found it necessary to repeat to himself his watchword: 'Keep smiling.'

As refugees from Nazi oppression, most of the genuine German and Austrian refugees were released from internment by mid-1941 or thereabouts. Many of those who had been deported to Canada or Australia returned to Britain when shipping became available, though some chose to stay where they were and make new lives for themselves there. After the war, the vast majority of the Jewish refugees either opted to remain in Britain or to emigrate onwards to the USA or Palestine; there was little or nothing for them to return to in Germany or Austria. Some of the political refugees, however, decided to return home in order to play a part in post-war reconstruction. Huyton Camp continued in existence as an alien internment camp until late 1941 – despite having originally been designated a short-term transit camp – and was next put to use as a prisoner of war camp, accommodating, among many others, Bert Trautmann of later football fame. The British policy of civilian internment continued on an increasingly small scale on the Isle of Man until September 1945 when the last of the internees (around 137 adults and accompanying children) were transferred to the mainland, to the Canon's Park Aliens Reception Centre, from where they were either repatriated or released.[30]

The internment of enemy aliens in the Second World War was neither the first occasion in the twentieth century that the policy had been implemented in wartime, nor would it be the last. As was noted above, enemy aliens were also interned in Britain during the First World War, the internees consisting largely of members of the German communities who had made their home here since the Victorian and Edwardian eras. During the Gulf War of 1991, enemy aliens were interned once again, in total 176 Iraqis and other Arabs, including seven Palestinians. In the words of David Cesarani and Tony Kushner: 'The tragedy of this episode was emphasized by the repetition, if on a smaller scale, of all the features and mistakes of the earlier internments.'[31] While in these three instances civilian internment was deployed as a wartime measure, internment has also been used in peacetime: between 1971 and 1975, arguably still more controversially, nearly 2,000 people, mostly Catholics, were interned in Northern Ireland. More recently, after 9/11 and the introduction of the 'War on Terror', a number of foreigners were held indefinitely in Belmarsh prison, consequently nicknamed the 'British Guantanamo', without charge or trial. The anti-alienism that lay at the heart of these unfortunate episodes continues to manifest itself today in the tough treatment of many asylum-seekers in Britain and in the deportation procedures of the British Home Office. Little has been learned, it would seem, from the suffering of waves of vulnerable men and women, including the German-speaking refugees from Hitler who are the main subject of this book, at the hands of the British authorities.

Notes

1   Estimates of refugee numbers vary from source to source. This figure is based on L. London, *Whitehall and the Jews 1933-1948: British Immigration Policy and the Holocaust* (Cambridge: Cambridge University Press, 2000), p. 12.

2   Figures given by Sir John Anderson to the House of Commons on 1 February and 1 March 1940, *Hansard*, HC, vol. 356, col. 1270; and vol. 357, col. 2410.

3   Anderson figures, *Hansard*, HC, 1 March 1940.

4   E. Spier, *The Protecting Power* (London: Skefington, 1951), p.20.

5   Dated 14 May 1940, The National Archives [TNA], FO 371/25189.

6   'There is More to be Done', *Daily Mail*, 24 May 1940, p.5.

7   For alien internment in the Second World War, see for example, F. Lafitte, *The Internment of Aliens* (Harmondsworth: Penguin, 1940; republished London: Libris,

1988); R. Stent, *A Bespattered Page? The Internment of 'His Majesty's Most Loyal Enemy Aliens'* (London: André Deutsch, 1980); P. and L. Gillman, *'Collar the Lot!' How Britain Interned and Expelled its Wartime Refugees* (London/Melbourne/ New York, Quartet, 1980); D. Cesarani and T. Kushner (eds), *The Internment of Aliens in Twentieth Century Britain* (London: Frank Cass, 1993); R. Dove (ed.), *'Totally Un-English?' Britain's Internment of Enemy Aliens in Two World Wars: Yearbook of the Research Centre for German and Austrian Exile Studies*, vol. 7 (Amsterdam: Rodopi, 2005); R. Pistol, *Internment during the Second World War: A Comparative Study of Great Britain and the USA* (London: Bloomsbury, 2017).

8   Lafitte, *op. cit*, pp. 101-02.

9   See minutes of 28 June 1940 and 29 June 1940, extracted from Knepler's Home Office file, in TNA, KV2/3820, 12a.

10   See C. Brinson and R. Dove, *A Matter of Intelligence: MI5 and the Surveillance of anti-Nazi Refugees, 1933-50* (Manchester: Manchester University Press, 2014), p. 151.

11   However, see J. Taylor, '"We Have More Than Enough": Conditions in Huyton Internment Camp in the Autumn and Early Winter of 1940', in *Journal of the Liverpool History Society*, 2009, pp. 99-108; J. Taylor (ed.), *Civilian Internment in Britain During WW2: Huyton Camp Eye-Witness Accounts*, Anglo-German Family History Society, 2012. See also J. Feather, *Art Behind Barbed Wire* (National Museums Liverpool, 2004).

12   O. Lehmann-Russbueldt, 'Alien Internment Camp Huyton-Liverpool: Erlebnisse und BeobachtungenzweierMonate', 3 September 1940, held at Deutsche Nationalbibliothek Frankfurt a. M., Deutsches Exilarchiv, Sternfeld Papers, EB 75/177, reproduced in English translation by J. Taylor in *Civilian Internment, op. cit.*, pp. 48-57. This paper was intended for Lord Lytton's Advisory Council on Aliens. See also accounts of internment in Huyton in H. Gal, *Music Behind Barbed Wire: A Diary of Summer 1940*, trans. A. Fox and E. Fox-Gal (London: Toccata, 2014); R. Neumann, unpublished internment diary, held at Österreichische Nationalbibliothek, Vienna, Neumann Papers, ser. N.21.608; Alfred Lomnitz, *'Never Mind, Mr. Lom! Or the Uses of Adversity* (London: Macmillan, 1941).

13   Lehmann-Russbueldt, in Taylor, *Civilian Internment*, pp. 48-49.

14   See C. Brinson, '"In the Exile of Internment" or "Von Versuchenauseiner Not eine Tugendzumachen"': German-speaking Women Interned by the British in the Second World War', in W. Niven and J. Jordan (eds), *Politics and Culture in Twentieth Century Germany* (Rochester, NY: Camden House, 2003), pp. 63-87.

15   Lehmann-Russbueldt in Taylor, *Civilian Internment*, p. 56.

16   *Ibid.*, pp. 51-52.

17   *Ibid.*, p. 51.

18   H.G. Wells, 'J'accuse', *Reynolds News*, 28 July 1940, p. 6.

19   *Hansard*, HC, vol. 362, cols. 1207-1306, 10 July 1940.

20   Lehmann-Russbueldt in Taylor, *Civilian Internment*, p.49.

21   *Hansard*, HL, vol. CXVI, col. 543, 12 June 1940.

22   *Ibid.*, col. 548.

23   On Bell's visit to Huyton see, for example, Bell to Pastor Franz Hildebrandt, 22 July 1940, Lambeth Palace Library, Bell Papers, vol.39, fol. 228; Bell to Rev. C.C. Griffiths, 23 July 1940, Bell papers, vol. 33, fol. 231.

24   See C. Brinson,'"Loyal to the Reich": National Socialists and Others in the Rushen Women's Internment Camp', in Dove, *'Totally Un-English?'*, op. cit., pp. 101-119

25 Anderson to Lytton, 13 August 1940, TNA, HO 213/1769.
26 'Matters emerging from Lytton's recent visit to Huyton', 12 August 1940, *ibid.*
27 Cmd. 6217, Cmd. 6223, Cmd. 6233.
28 See Snell Report, 25 November 1940, TNA, WP (40) 463, CAB 66/13; P. and L. Gillman, *'Collar the lot! How Britain Interned and Expelled its Wartime Refugees* (London/Melbourne/New York: Quartet, 1980), p. 98.
29 See R. Dove, '"KZ auf englisch": Robert Neumann's Internment Diary', in C. Brinson, R. Dove, M. Malet and J. Taylor, *'England Aber wo liegtes?' Deutsche und österreichische Emigranten in Großbritannien, 1933-1945* (Munich: iudicium, 1996).
30 Memorandum concerning the closing of WY Camp Port Erin, n.d. [August 1945], TNA, HO 215/479.
31 Cesarani and Kushner, *op. cit.*, p. 214.

2

Portrait of a Man: Wilhelm Hollitscher and Hugo Dachinger

'Just as I am and not as I appear to the world'

On 28 June 2016 Ben Uri Gallery and Museum was delighted to acquire from auction in London a distinctive head-and-shoulders portrait of a white-haired man with piercing blue eyes. Strikingly fresh, even after almost 80 years, the watercolour and gouache on newsprint was signed 'Dachinger', inscribed 'Huyton' and dated '40'. Ben Uri's curators immediately recognised it as one of a series of portraits made during British internment of so-called enemy aliens in the early years of the Second World War, by the Austrian émigré artist Hugo (Puck) Dachinger (1908-1995); however, the identity of the sitter remained tantalisingly unknown.

Dating from this difficult moment in British wartime history,[1] the portrait was accessioned to complement Ben Uri's permanent collection of over 1,400 artworks which focusses particularly on the contribution of émigré artists in Britain from 1900 onwards.[2] Ben Uri itself was founded in 1915 in London's East End ghetto during the First World War by Jewish émigré artists and designers who had fled the Russian Pale of Settlement and were unable to access the cultural bastions of the British art establishment.[3] Now in its second century, Ben Uri has continued to draw on the Jewish émigré narrative as a key template for its activities, with a particular interest in the second wave who fled Nazism in Europe between 1933-45. Furthermore, most recently, Ben Uri has broadened its strategy to encompass the wider refugee experience in Britain and its contribution to British visual culture since 1900, under the auspices of the newly-formed Ben Uri Research Unit.[4]

Prior to this significant purchase, Dachinger was already represented in the Ben Uri collection with two later pen and ink drawings: *Paul Hamann's Drawing Class*, 1962[5] and *Bell Street Market*, 1977,[6] depicting different aspects of the artist's later life in London.

Paul Hamann's Drawing Class, Hugo Dachinger, 1962. Ben Uri Collection © The Estate of Hugo Dachinger.

Bell Street Market, Hugo Dachinger, 1977. Ben Uri Collection © The Estate of Hugo Dachinger.

The earlier work referenced Dachinger's close ties with the refugee network which he maintained following his release from internment. Hamann,[7] a noted sculptor from Hamburg and pupil of Rodin, had been interned on the Isle of Man at Hutchinson camp – the so-called 'artists' camp – along with German expressionists, Ludwig Meidner and Erich Kahn; the Austrian sculptors, Siegfried Charoux and Georg Ehrlich; and Kurt Schwitters, the renowned Dadaist from Hanover (who painted Hamann's portrait in camp), among others.[8] Following his release, Hamann held private art classes with his wife, Hilde, in St John's Wood, where many émigrés regularly met. He was also a founder member of the refugee

Photo of Hugo and Meta Dachinger and their daughter Miriam. © Dachinger Estate, courtesy Suppan Fine Arts, Vienna.[9]

organisation, the Free German League of Culture,[10] geographically rooted close to Finchley Road, which was often referred to by local bus conductors as *Finchleystrasse* in the immediate post-war period, given the significant number of German speakers who settled locally. The second sketch depicted Bell Street Market, just off Lisson Grove, further south in NW1; with its mixture of junk and vintage stalls, it was a popular émigré haunt. In both sketches, with a few deft strokes in pen and ink, Dachinger has conjured up lively characters and period atmosphere.

The general details of Dachinger's biography were also well known within Ben Uri: he was born in Gmunden in Austria, studied graphic design in Leipzig, Germany, returned to Austria to work, fled to England after the *Anschluss* and married and had a family in London, where he eventually died in exile. In the decades after his death, his significance as an émigré artist with Austrian heritage was receiving renewed recognition in his homeland, with the publication in 2007 of the monograph *Hugo Puck Dachinger – Innovationsgeist im Exil* by Martin Suppan of Galerie Suppan, Vienna.[11]

As with many Jewish artists and designers, following the rise of National Socialism from 1933 and the imposition of anti-Semitic laws, Dachinger was eventually unable to make a living in his chosen profession. He had patented a system of moveable type in Germany and worked for the international Viennese publishers C Barth Verlag from 1934, but in the wake of the annexation of Austria in 1938, his career was effectively over – from 1 January 1939 no Jew was allowed to be a practicing advertising professional. Escaping to London on 19 June 1938 and sustained by business contacts with Saville & Co, Dachinger established his own company in exile: Transposter Advertising Ltd. However, a second professional blow was rapidly dealt – with the outbreak of war, as an enemy alien, he was no longer permitted to work in London.

Nevertheless, although graphic design as a job was denied to him, Dachinger was able to channel his creativity as an accomplished draughtsman and painter – albeit as a rather unfashionable expressionist. As one of around 300 émigré artists and designers who took refuge in Britain from Nazism, Dachinger was not only faced with the daily challenges of living in an unfamiliar country with an unfamiliar language, but with the additional problem that 'German' art (there was a certain blurring, in the public eye, of distinctions between German-speaking nationalities) was currently little known and unfashionable. The British public – those who had any interest in the subject – preferred their modern art to come from France, without the darker mood, weighty introspection and dramatic palette of expressionism. Even those artists who had been well established in Germany and Austria found it difficult to find a new audience and to secure patronage. 'It would not be untrue to say that to the general public in Great Britain, modern German art is totally unknown',[12] wrote the critic and art historian Herbert Read in his introduction to the important 1938 exhibition 'Modern German Art' held at the New Burlington Gallery in central London. The exhibition and accompanying catalogue showcased the work of a range of artists, a number of whom had been included in the infamous 1937 Degenerate Art (*Entartete Kunst*)[13] exhibition which was currently touring Germany – designed to highlight those artists who were publicly vilified by the National Socialists: Jews, left-wingers and modernists (but whose work, in fact, was often collected by the regime).

In June 1940, following the invasion of France, newly-elected Prime Minister, Winston Churchill, issued a directive to 'Collar the lot!', calling for all so-called enemy aliens to be interned, regardless of whether they had been victims of Nazi oppression in their own homelands. Dachinger was duly swept up in the mass internment of around 27,000 'enemy aliens', mostly Jewish refugees, who were interned in hastily adapted, short term transit camps across the British mainland and in more permanent locations on the Isle of Man and Commonwealth destinations in Australia and Canada.

Dachinger subsequently spent five months incarcerated at Huyton Camp, Liverpool, located within the recently built Woolfall Heath corporation housing estate, divided from the outside world by an eight-metre high barbed wire fence. Up to 5,000 internees were held at any one time, the majority, Jewish victims of Nazi persecution, though a small percentage claimed allegiance to the Reich.[14] Houses intended for a single family were crammed with up to 12 occupants, military barracks for 20 had 44 people crammed in and the rest were in tents.

Other notable émigré artists at Huyton included Samson Schames, Martin Bloch, Walter Nessler, Alfred Lomnitz, Reinhold Nagele and the aforementioned Ludwig Meidner. Meidner, surprisingly, declared himself in captivity to be: '[…] healthy and have become young again, look as if I am in my early forties and draw portraits all day, including commissions, as well as landscapes when the weather is good, for there is also nature to be found in this architecturally well-designed camp, which is a modern workers' estate and will in the future resume this function again.'[15] Many internees, including Lomnitz, were released directly from Huyton, while others, such as Bloch, Meidner and Dachinger, were transferred onwards to the Isle of Man or abroad.

The Tent, Huyton. Walter Nessler, 1940. The Walker, National Museums Liverpool. © Artist's Estate

As with the majority of Huyton portraits produced by a range of artists – and, indeed, with many portraits made during internment in general – the identity of Dachinger's sitter had become lost over time. However, through an extraordinary set of coincidences, this was suddenly and unexpectedly revealed. On 15 March 2018, Ben Uri's Chairman, David Glasser, was interviewed on BBC news for a sound bite about the potential impact of Brexit on museums in Britain. He happened to be filmed seated in front of the newly-acquired portrait, which featured in Ben Uri's spring 2018 exhibition: *Out of Austria,* marking the 80th anniversary of both the *Anschluss* and *Kristallnacht*[16] – events which had impelled so many Jewish refugees to flee Germany and Austria, and had led to the establishment of the British *Kindertransport* initiative in 1938, which enabled 10,000 Jewish children and adolescents to come to Britain. The news segment was viewed by one of the sitter's granddaughters, Ines Newman, who wasted no time in contacting Ben Uri. Ines was able to confirm that the portrait, painted in the third month of the artist's internment at Huyton, depicts Austrian Jewish refugee Wilhelm Hollitscher (1873-1943), father of Lisbeth

Oppenheimer (née Hollitscher), mother of Hannah, Ralph, Margaret, Ines and Susan.

Detailed entries from the diary of Wilhelm Hollitscher from Huyton and letters from immediately after his release, in conjunction with Dachinger's portraits, provide a clear account not only of the conditions of captivity and artistic endeavour behind the wire, but of the relationship between émigré sitter and émigré artist, and something of the wider émigré cultural scene in 1940s London.

Hollitscher wrote his first English diary entry on 13 June 1939, almost exactly a year before he was interned, describing his initial stay in Salford prior to moving south to Petts Wood in Kent, where he remained – apart from internment – until his death in 1943. In mid-July 1940, now in Huyton, he described his first meeting with Dachinger;

> In the Shepton Road, there lives a young painter, Dachinger, by name and appearance a pure Aryan type who has painted the walls of his five person occupied room with very good naked women – a family picture! His room-mates have made a table out of stolen wood, an armchair for the house father, three chairs and a self-made saw. They are a lot of jolly young lads, four from Vienna, one German – I think if I were young I would manage to do some useful and good things. But now I am an old invalid observer. Today it is three weeks since my arrest, time races by.[17]

Hollitscher was among the circle of middle-class intellectuals, writers and artists with whom Dachinger mixed in camp. Dachinger, as with many of his fellow artist internees across a range of camps, made many distinctive portraits (such as those by Kurt Schwitters in Hutchinson on the Isle of Man, who created many memorable images, for which he established a sliding scale of charges, depending on the complexity of the composition). The Hollitscher portrait is instantly recognisable stylistically as a Dachinger – particularly when compared to other portraits in Jessica Feather's *Art Behind Barbed Wire*, an exhibition and accompanying catalogue presented in 2004 by the Walker Gallery, Liverpool, which featured artwork by Dachinger and German émigré artist Walter Nessler as Second World War internees (and by Thomas Burke (1906-45) as a Liverpool-born prisoner of war held in Germany during the First World War).[18] Dachinger's portraits therein range from empathetic, instantly recognisable likenesses to more modernist, semi-abstract interpretations, some with the distinctive graphic qualities of a billboard advert or poster, such as *Jooss: 20 Jahre für*

Jooss: 20 Jahre für den Tanz (Jooss: 20 Years of Dance) Hugo Dachinger and Fritz Rosen, Huyton 1940. The Walker, National Museums Liverpool.© Artist's Estate

den Tanz, made in collaboration with fellow internee, Fritz Rosen (1890-1980).[19]

Dachinger is also represented by more complex, multi-figured genre scenes depicting everyday life in camp (such as Plate 6 *Dinner in Campton Park*, and Plate 2 *Potato Peelers*) and its tedium, along with more brooding camp-scapes, executed in a sombre palette, in which the composition is divided by the ever-present angular motifs of perimeter fence, strands of wire and watchtowers. Beyond a basic desire to represent the daily privations (see plate 8A *Dead End* and Plate 8B *Perimeter Fence Under Red Sky*), petty humiliations (see Plate 4 *Two Internees Bowing in Front of an Officer*) and the sheer boredom of internment (see Plate 2A *Waiting Waiting*), Dachinger also conveyed more complex psychological issues faced by the internees, wrestling with their loss of identity, detained by the very country in which they had sought refuge.

Despite the poor conditions and overcrowding at Huyton, Dachinger's overall artistic output was extremely prolific and, as well as portraiture, landscapes, genre scenes and posters, he also produced stylised nudes as decoration for the camp's very own Café Vienna. However, traditional art materials were often in short supply, and the artists became, by necessity, increasingly resourceful.[20] If paints and brushes were hard to come by, other items were substituted for drawing implements and other ingredients were mixed to make alternative pigments. Twigs were burnt to create sticks of charcoal; short beard hairs were plucked to use for brushes, and paints were made from brick dust or vegetable juice ground with linseed oil or olive oil

Line of Internees Following a Soldier with Rifle. Hugo Dachinger, Huyton 1940. The Walker, National Museums Liverpool.© Artist's Estate

from sardine cans. In the Hollitscher portrait, Dachinger appears to have used varying transparencies of watercolour and gouache, to make the pigments more or less vivid, perhaps even mixing with toothpaste to make the hair seem whiter and more opaque. And – as it exemplifies – any shortage of drawing paper was easily overcome, with the artists becoming avid re-purposers of old newspapers as suitable supports for painting. Newsprint could be primed with gelatine from boiled-down bones mixed with flour, a method which left daily accounts of war and diplomacy tantalisingly visible beneath the composition. Certain papers were regarded as more suitable than others, as a piece on Dachinger in *Picture Post* later noted his preference for *The Times*.[21]

Semi-visible headlines inevitably lent a particular graphic and narrative quality to artworks executed on newsprint. Adverts, photographs, cartoons, columns of type and individual words or phrases, all drew the eye and were often incorporated by Dachinger to great effect, no doubt facilitated by his background in advertising (see Plate 6 *Dinner in Campton Park: Vitamins enlisted to win the war,*). *Portrait of a Man Wearing Blue Shirt and Red Tie* (Plate 5) is made all the more powerful by the inclusion of a single large print word 'Search' in an advert in the lower right corner. There is also a poignancy in Hollitscher's portrait: in the right hand column of text, the phrase 'Domestic Situations Wanted' is clearly visible – menial household work was often the only hope of passage for many privileged or over-qualified female refugees.[22]

Over a fortnight in August 1940, Hollitscher recorded various sittings in his diary, the first taking place on 5 August. 'Hugo Dachinger is making a pastel picture of me, this afternoon was my first sitting, he says that I don't laugh and he finds my head interesting'. He recorded completion of the portrait on 8 August:

> Last sitting for painter Dachinger – colourful, quite modern style. It is interesting for me because he sees me such as I am and not as I appear to the world. I look like a Prussian general – a strange resemblance to a photo that Hansl took of me after my first operation: more severe, more sombre, more suffering. My look – sharp features with high cheekbones. Dachinger wants to make a second sketch as does his friend, who, according to how he describes me, is also interested artistically in me.

The newspaper in the Ben Uri portrait is dated 6 August 1940, so perhaps it dates from this second sitting – though this cannot be verified absolutely.

Hollitscher's overcoat has a military feel, reinforced by the visible headline 'Air Fights in Many Spheres', but it carries no specific insignia. Its large lapels suggest that it is not the 'overall suit' which he received in a parcel in late July and mentioned in a diary entry. The distinctive blue and yellow palette can be found in other Huyton portraits by Dachinger, such as *Portrait of a man in a checked jacket, reading* and *Portrait of a man in a blue sweater and brown jacket*.[23] Dachinger's empathetic treatment of his fellow internees contrasts with his sharply satirical, sometimes cartoonish works featuring camp officers.

A second portrait was begun on 10 August 1940 and the friend referred to may have been the German graphic artist, fellow internee, Fritz Rosen (1890-1980) who subsequently worked on British anti-Nazi propaganda posters. The entry for 11 August 1940 records that: 'Dachinger made a sketch of me yesterday on newspaper working directly with colour. He certainly has talent- an immediate impression, not a true likeness, caught with concentrated observation. He intends to make another, Rosen was not present'. A third portrait was recorded on 14 August 1940: 'Dachinger has made a third coloured sketch of me, I think the best yet. He says he is beginning to know me now that he has discovered my intellectual head and I, simple fool, have discovered it too.' – and a final portrait on 21 August: 'Dachinger made the fourth sketch of me today; sitting, the whole upper body. The head, in my opinion, is the most successful yet. He gave me a sample of a beautifully created invitation by him and Rosen to their art exhibition and invited me for Friday to a sausage feast.' An unidentified black and white reproduction illustrated in the Suppan monograph possibly shows one of the remaining three portraits, with Hollitscher wearing the so-called overall suit but, unfortunately, the newsprint date is not legible in the reproduction.[24]

Dachinger duly presented Hollitscher with his latest portrait sketch on 26 August 1940, 'which is generally approved as good – a nice memento'. Indeed, portraits taken away from internment can often serve as important documents of captivity, sometimes providing a vital clue to the identity of both artist and sitter, particularly for the Manx men's camps, where the records of internment are surprisingly patchy. Notable examples include the caricature of Onchan camp impresario, Jack Bilbo (Hugo Baruch, 1907- 67), self-styled 'Artist, Author, Sculptor, Art Dealer, Philosopher, Psychologist, Traveller and a Modernist Fighter for Humanity'[25] by Heinz Kiewe, which depicts Bilbo as *Jumping Jack Bilbo*, the great puppet master of Onchan, with trademark pipe and a barbed wire belt, pulling strings connected variously to politics, the Popular University, uniforms and

'Caaaabaret'; those by Kurt Schwitters; by the young Austrian émigré, Ernst Eisenmayer (1920-2018) and by less well-known figures such as Schreck, whose presence in internment may only be recorded through portraiture – their own biographies often remaining obscure.

Hollitscher's diary entry for 30 August 1940 references the art exhibition at Huyton, held just prior to his release. This was one of the earliest internment camp exhibitions. Both Hutchinson and Onchan camps on the Isle of Man – each with their own impressario and distinguished roster of artists – and Mooragh camp, to where Dachinger was later transferred, held well-publicised exhibitions in autumn 1940.

> Yesterday afternoon there was the opening of the exhibition, *'Art behind the Wire'*, in a new corrugated iron shed[...] The presentation of the pictures was excellent with paper screens – sections – obviously in the camp these were primitive measures. Dachinger has his own small room. My picture and Kramers's and his mood sketches – everything on newspaper – much in pencil, charcoal, pastels and water colour. Some very good portraits of A. D. and Sch. Very witty caricatures of Rot, Müller, Baier. Rosen has made a placard titled *'War means only Peace'*, on newspaper with water colours, the British Lion in an aggressive pose pressing down on German planes with his front paw; and a fantastic caricature called *'Censor's Constipation'*, a naked overweight man sitting on a pot. A lot of people say that Dachinger is the best and most talented.[26]

From Huyton, Dachinger was sent in October 1940 to Mooragh Camp at Ramsey on the Isle of Man, until his release in January 1941, and from where he continued to produce artworks. In November he held an exhibition in the camp of his internment drawings, entitled *Art Behind Barbed Wire*, advertised with a striking poster of his own design, foregrounding a single barb of wire and a stylised eye. Following his release, an exhibition of the same name and utilising the same poster design (see back cover of this book) was held at London's Redfern Gallery in Cork Street in central London (where it is still located 80 years later and continues to represent a number of distinguished émigré artists). The exhibition, which ran from 9-26 April 1941, was supported by the Free Austrian Movement in Great Britain (FAM), an Austrian refugee organisation with 7,000 members and a roster of high-profile émigré patrons including Elias Canetti and Oskar Kokoschka.[27]

Hollitscher's letters to his daughter after his release highlight the continuing relationship with Dachinger. Friendships forged in captivity were often deep and lasting, and enabled émigrés to create significant informal networks of fellow internees post-internment. For artists, contacts with their émigré peers and with émigré gallerists such as Jack Bilbo, who opened his Modern Art Gallery in central London in 1941 and provided much support for émigré exhibitors, were particularly meaningful. Bilbo (born Hugo Baruch) had been the flamboyant impresario encouraging artistic endeavour in Onchan camp on the Isle of Man, hosting two interned art exhibitions in his 'cabin' during autumn 1940. A self-taught artist, his gallery, which was first located at 12 Baker Street, exhibited a fascinating roster of émigré and interned artists, such as Dachinger, Kokoschka, Schames and Schwitters, along with more mainstream works by French masters such as Degas, Gauguin and Rodin. Bilbo claimed that he 'didn't let fame or obscurity decide which picture should be accepted or not',[28] and the gallery remained a rare beacon of exhibition activity whilst much of London remained closed.

On 14 March 1941 Hollitscher recorded Dachinger's release – although the artist's 62-year old father, inexplicably, remained interned – along with an invitation to Dachinger's one-man exhibition at the Redfern Gallery which Hollitscher 'will attend if at all possible'.

The Redfern catalogue reprised the now familiar title: *Art Behind Barbed Wire* and the stylised motif based on the wire in its top left corner. Of 40 exhibits, more than a quarter were portraits of some sort, based on their titles, which included: *Philosopher; Once an art critic in Vienna* and *The man who never saw Germany.*[29] The titles also suggest that the artworks were not only from Huyton, but from earlier transit experiences at Kempton racecourse and from later internment at Mooragh camp. The exhibition was marked by a small paragraph in the *Jewish Chronicle*, the weekly paper of the Anglo-Jewish community:

> A young Austrian refugee painter, Hugo Dachinger, who has just been released from internment, is giving an exhibition of his paintings which he executed while in internment. The exhibition, which is to be called 'Art Behind Barbed Wire' will open at the Redfern Gallery. 20, Cork Street, W.I, over the week-end and will continue for a month.[30]

Hollitscher's dairy entry for 18 April 1941 notes that his intended visit to the exhibition was thwarted by air raids: 'Very heavy bombing in the night.

[...]. Had to cancel dentist – trains were not running. Wanted to use my stay in London to go to the Redfern Gallery to see the exhibition '7 months in an English internment camp, impressions' painted by Hugo Dachinger'. Hollitscher was more successful a week later and artist and sitter dined at a 'small eatery in Soho in continental style'.[31] Three weeks later Hollitscher wrote that, following efforts on the part of Dachinger, he hopes his diary will be published:

> I lent my diary from Huyton to the young painter Dachinger[...] He gave the diary to Rosner a writer and friend of his and he said he'd never been so moved for years, 'everything is so natural and humane – it is the work of a typical Viennese – the work of a clever old gentleman' – what nonsense, if I meet this Rosner I will tell him what a cheek he has to call me an old man. But the best thing is that Rosner is trying to get this published with pictures and illustrations by Dachinger.[32]

Confirming the identity of Rosner has also been an interesting exercise – having initially drawn a blank, a chance visit to the launch of a book on Hungarian émigré artists held at the Hungarian Cultural Centre in London in spring 2018, revealed a Charles Rosner (Károly Rosner, 1902-1972), a Hungarian-born émigré author and publisher who commuted between Budapest and London during the 1930s. An energetic and patriotic cultural facilitator, he variously worked for the BBC's Hungarian Service, was Hungarian 'editor' for *Studio* magazine, instigator of an exhibition of Hungarian graphic art in London in 1943, and owner of the Sylvan Press, which specialised in books on typography, design and printing, and the art of the poster and dust jacket, concerns which of course dovetailed perfectly with Dachinger's own professional and creative interests.

On 12 June 1941 Hollitscher recorded that '[...] Friday I spent the whole day with the family of Dachinger and in the afternoon Rosner came [...] Rosner really wants to publish my diary and Dachinger wants to do 12 pen drawings but he wants to wait until circumstances are more favourable. Dachinger told me that an article about his exhibition has appeared in the *Picture Post* together with my portrait.' *Picture Post* was a weekly illustrated news magazine, renowned for its photo-journalism, a particular way of humanising the war, and a distinctly émigré pedigree. Co-founded in 1938 by another Hungarian, Stefan Lorant, with British publisher Sir Edward Hulton, it employed a number of émigré photo

Photo of Charles Rosner (Károly Rosner, 1902-1972) reproduced with permission from Frankie Elliott (known also as artist Frankie Partridge)

journalists, including Ken (Kurt) Hutton and Francis Reiss and had been requested as reading material by the Huyton internees.[33]

Three months later, on 12 September, Hollitscher recorded that his portrait by Dachinger featured in the latest issue of *Picture Post*, captioned: 'Portrait of an anonymous internee', in the so-called Picture Medley section, described at the top of the double-page spread as: 'Picture Stories in miniature. Single pictures out of series which in peacetime, would have had one, two or three pages to themselves.'[34] A separate caption noted that Dachinger used 'a brush made from his own hair and newspaper for canvas. Says he gets his best results on the front page of "*The Times*" but, if hard put to it, could muddle through with a "*Daily Telegraph*" or "*Manchester Guardian*". Big headline papers e.g. "*Daily Express*," unsuitable. Large lettering shouts through paint.'[35]

However, despite this publicity and Rosner's previous enthusiasm, for whatever reason, the illustrated diary project seems to have foundered, with a disappointing update recorded by Hollitscher at the end of October:

> [...] Dachinger told me that the writer Rosner, who is now employed at the BBC, has left his flat, he doesn't know to where, and he hasn't seen him. Rosner has my plan of the house and various caricatures and drawings and various unique curiosities. As far as I can judge, what are called 'Valuable contemporary artefacts' have been lost to posterity, so it is an inconspicuous end to the whole affair.'[36]

Hollitscher and Dachinger, nevertheless, remained friends, meeting sporadically, and Hollitscher evidently retained an interest in Austrian culture in exile. On 8 November 1941 he described visiting London: 'to see an exhibition of Austrian painters which closed on Tuesday. There were four pictures of Dachinger exhibited'. This may have been the first annual exhibition of Austrian artists held in the premises of the Austrian Women's Voluntary Workers in London, part of the FAM.[37]

Early in the new year, however, there was clearly a postscript to the diary publication debacle, as Hollitscher noted: 'Met up with Dachinger who had previously had supper with the author Rosner from whom I received back my diary notes from Huyton. Rosner and his author wife and Dachinger think that my notes are better than this book *Never Mind, Mr. Lom* which made me feel like a self-important peacock and I came home and buried them under completed writings.'[38] The reference to *Never Mind, Mr. Lom* is particularly significant. Alfred Lomnitz was a German émigré artist and designer who, as previously mentioned, was also interned

Front cover of *Never Mind, Mr. Lom* by Alfred Lomnitz (London, Macmillan & Co Ltd, 1941), reproduced with permission of the Lansdale family.

at Huyton. He had written an earlier account of interment under the title *Never Mind, Mr. Lom* (the cheery parting comment from his char lady, as he was bundled away by the police), which was published by Macmillan in 1941.

The publication presented a somewhat sanitised and positive account of the Huyton experience, interwoven with charming sketches of life in captivity (although the cover design included a lone figure confronting a forbidding barbed-wire perimeter fence), perhaps in an attempt to reassure the British public that internment wasn't so bad after all.[39] Hollitscher added to the entry the following heartfelt remarks about the diary and his wishes for it, now that the Dachinger/Rosner project has failed:

> To be truthful I didn't do anything different in Huyton than I have for decades: daily entries, not just about my personal experiences, but also my thoughts about general happenings, about books, about discoveries, about the sub-conscious. In these reflections, I leave myself to you, your children and your children's children as a human being. So long as I live, no one is to have access to my diary but the Huyton experience was such that I thought it should be read by a few friends and particularly by you, my children. And this very intention has been thwarted since I cannot under the present circumstances send it to you. I will have to wait till the war is over.[40]

The following autumn Hollitscher recorded a trip to London where he:

> Visited the Dachinger exhibition in the 'Modern Art Gallery' founded by author and painter Jack Bilbo in the first floor of an old house in Baker Street with the sole aim and purpose of helping art to survive and of giving the artist and the public a possibility of doing their part in the intellectual fight against dictatorial reactionism. Dachinger's paintings veer between pre-Raphaelite and cubist, he has sold 4 of them.[41]

There may have been a conscious effort on Dachinger's part to present a variety of artistic styles in the hope of maximising sales. Certainly, Bilbo had no preference for a single style or aesthetic, but rather sought to shake up the established London gallery scene with his firm commitment to selling work 'from the artistic point of view'.

Hollitscher's last reference to Dachinger was made the following spring, on 24 April 1943, when he was a witness at Dachinger's marriage to fellow émigré artist, Meta Guttmann. He noted that both artists expressed a wish to paint him in a style which he described as falling somewhere between 'Impressionist and pre-Raphaelite', but because Hollitscher was unwell – he had a history of poor health – there would only be two sittings. Sadly, it seems likely that these never took place.

A month earlier, on the fourth anniversary of his arrival in England, in March 1943, Hollitscher wrote movingly that he is grateful for four years of a 'blessed old age' and for the fact that his children and grandchildren are safe and healthy. He mentions heart troubles, difficulties in sleeping and cramps. The diaries close rather abruptly on 6 October 1943.

There is, however, a further postscript in the 'life' of the portrait: prior to its identification, and prior to the concept of this volume, the portrait featured as a striking cover image for Anthony Grenville's 2017 publication: *Encounters with Albion: Britain and the British in Texts by Jewish Refugees from Nazism.*[42] And with appropriate circularity, it is the efforts of Wilhelm's remaining grandchildren in England – as the 80th anniversary of internment in Britain is marked in 2020 – that have ensured that both diary extracts and Dachinger's marvellous portrait (now suitably identified), are brought together so prominently in this publication.

Notes

1   See chapter in this book by C. Brinson and D. Cesarani and T. Kushner (eds), *The Internment of Aliens in Twentieth Century Britain* (London and New York: Routledge, 1993).
2   https://www.benuri.org.uk/collection/
3   D. Mazower, 'Lazar Berson and the origins of the Ben Uri Art Society', in G. Rathbone (ed.), *The Ben Uri Story from Art Society to Museum*, (London: Ben Uri Gallery, The London Jewish Museum of Art, 2001), pp. 37-58.
4   https://www.benuri.org.uk/emigre-artists-research-unit/
5   https://www.benuricollection.org.uk/search_result.php?item_id=1048
    The sculptor and German émigré Paul Hamann (1891–1973) and his artist wife Hilde (1898–1987), both former members of the Hamburger Secession, settled in England in 1937, after living in artists' colonies in Worpswede and Paris. Hamann invented a painless technique for life masks and exhibited at the Free German League of Culture's Exhibition of Twentieth Century Art (New Burlington Galleries, 1938); both were included in the First Group Exhibition of German, Austrian, Czechoslovakian Painters and Sculptors (Wertheim Gallery, 1939, co-organised by the Austrian Centre and the FGLC).
6   *Bell Street Market*, 1977 Pen and ink on paper, 28 x 39 cm. Signed and dated (lower right) 'D H 1977', Inscribed. Ben Uri Collection.
7   See warthmillsproject.com for a more detailed account of Hamann's experience in British internment camps.

8   See K. Hinrichsen, 'Visual Art Behind the Wire' in D. Cesarani and T. Kushner (eds), *The Internment of Aliens in Twentieth Century Britain* (London and New York: Routledge, 1993), pp. 188-209.

9   M. Suppan (ed.) *Hugo Puck Dachinger (1908-1995), Innovationsgeist im Exil.* The Spirit of Innovation in Exile, Monograph with catalogue raisonnés (Vienna: Suppan Gallery, 2007). http://www.suppanfinearts.com/en/publications/werkverzeichnisse/hugo-dachinger.

10   C. Brinson and R. Dove (eds), *Politics by Other Means: The Free German League of Culture in London, 1939-1946* (London and New York: Vallentine Mitchell, 2021).

11   See Suppan, *Hugo Puck Dachinger.*

12   H. Read, 'Introduction' in P. Thoene, *Modern German Art* (Harmondsworth: Penguin Books, 1938), p. 7. The exhibition was originally scheduled to run from 8-31 July 1938 but was extended due to popular demand. It featured the work of 31 'degenerate' artists.

13   The exhibition was first held in Munich from 19 July to 30 November 1937and featured 650 paintings, sculptures and prints by 112 artists, who were primarily German, though important non-German modernists such as Picasso, Mondrian and Chagall were also included. The exhibition toured subsequently in Germany and Austria.

14   J. Taylor (ed.), *Civilian Internment in Britain during WW2: Huyton Camp Eye-witness Accounts,* (Anglo-German Family History Society Publications, 2012).

15   Letter from Ludwig Meidner to Hilde and Walter Rosenbaum dated 24 September 1940, Institut Mathildenhöhe, Städtische Kunstsammlung Darmstadt, at Stadtarchiv Darmstadt, ST 45 Meidner 1176.

16   https://www.artforum.com/artguide/ben-uri-gallery-and-museum-14269/out-of-austria-marking-the-80th-anniversary-of-the-anschluss-152330 Accessed 19 February 2020.

17   Diary entry for 16 July 1940.

18   J. Feather (ed.), *Art Behind Barbed Wire,* (National Museums Liverpool, 2004), published for the exhibition 'Art Behind Barbed Wire', 26 February-3 May 2004.

19   Ibid.

20   R. Dickson, S MacDougall and U. Smalley, '"Astounding and Encouraging": High and Low Art produced in Internment on the Isle of Man during the Second World War' in G. Carr, H. Mytum(eds), *Cultural Heritage and Prisoners of War: Creativity Behind Barbed Wire* (London and New York: Routledge, 2012), pp. 186-206.

21   See note 34.

22   Anthony Grenville: 'Underpaid, Underfed, and Overworked: Refugees in Domestic Service' in *AJR Journal,* December 2008.

23   J. Feather (ed.), *Art Behind Barbed Wire,* pp. 26-27.

24   M. Suppan, WN60, p.201.

25   R. Dickson, S MacDougall and U. Smalley, '"Astounding and Encouraging": High and Low Art produced in Internment on the Isle of Man during the Second World War', p. 199.

26   Diary entry for 30 August 1940.

27   S. Frank (ed.), *Young Austria: Osterreicherinnenim Britschen Exil 1938-1947* (Wien: OGB Verlag, 2012).

28   J Bilbo, *Jack Bilbo* (London: The Modern Art Gallery, 1948), p. 255-276.

29   Catalogue courtesy Redfern Gallery archives.

30   *Jewish Chronicle,* 4 April 1941, p. 18.

31 Letter dated 25 April 1941.

32 Letter dated 14 May 1941.

33 W. Weinke, "'It is the spaces between the notes that give the sound". Von Hamburg, über London, New York nach Australien: Der Fotograf Francis Reiss' in M. Malet, R. Dickson, S. MacDougall, A. Nyburg (eds), *Applied Arts in British Exile from 1933: Changing Visual and Material Culture*, The Yearbook of the Research Centre for German and Austrian Exile Studies, Vol. 19 (Leiden/Boston: Brill Rodopi, 2019), pp. 107-131.

34 *Picture Post*, pp. 24-25 Dated 13 Sept 1941.

35 Ibid.

36 Letter dated 31 October 1941.

37 W. Muchitsch, *Österreicherim Exil: Großbritannien 1938 – 1945 Eine Dokumentation* (Wien: Österreichischer Bundesverlag, 1992), p. 471.

38 Letter dated for 16 January 1942.

39 A. Lomnitz, *Never Mind, Mr. Lom* (London: Macmillan and Co. Ltd, 1941).

40 Letter dated for 16 January 1942.

41 Letter dated for 30 October 1942. See J. Bilbo, *Jack Bilbo An Autobiography* (Leeds/London: E.J. Arnold & Sons Ltd. / The Modern Art Gallery Ltd., 1948).

42 A. Grenville, *Encounters with Albion: Britain and the British in Texts by Jewish Refugees from Nazism* (Cambridge: Modern Humanities Research Association/Legenda, 2017).

3

Wilhelm Hollitscher: 'Keep Smiling'

Ines Newman

It is one of the main regrets in my life that I never met my grandfather, Wilhelm Hollitscher. He died in October 1943, four years before I was born. My family were in Egypt, where they lived until 1949, at the time of his death. My eldest sister, Hannah, did meet him when she was a nineteen month-old baby, as my mother took her to Vienna in the autumn of 1938, after the *Anschluss*. My father sent my mother increasingly desperate letters telling her to come back before it was too late and, much to his relief, she returned a couple of weeks before *Kristallnacht*. Our grandfather continued to write regularly to his daughter Lisl and, by the time he came to England and Hannah was two, he wrote at least once a week to her (Hannele as he called her), creating a magical little story for her or relating an anecdote and asking a couple of simple questions to which she replied by dictation. He was a distinct presence in her early life. Hannah has a clear picture of our mother receiving the news of his death and weeping, with the telegram in her hand.

Our mother died in 1954 so, by the time we were curious, we had no one to answer our questions about our maternal grandparents. It has therefore been a pleasure to discover his diary and to work on the translation of this and his letters to both Lisl and his son Hansl. What has emerged is a kind, positive, warm and charismatic man whom it has been a delight to get to know.

To understand him fully it is important to comprehend the constraints that poor Jews in the Austro-Hungarian Empire were under up to the late nineteenth century. We are very fortunate in having a 'memoir' that my great grandfather, Simon Hollitscher (1839-1927), wrote between 1912 and 1917. One of the common traits in my family is a compulsion to write which provides a rich source of historical material. This short biography of my grandfather therefore starts with a brief history of the Jews in Vienna and Wilhelm's ancestors.

Wilhelm Hollitscher, 1/10/1933, black and white photograph, © Oppenheimer family

From Hapsburg Empire to Austria

The Hapsburg Monarchs were powerful rulers. From 1438 until 1806 (with the exception of 1742–1745) the head of the House of Habsburg was also the Holy Roman Emperor, During the regime of Leopold I(who reigned from 1658–1705), the Jews faced frequent persecution and were deported from different areas, including a deportation from Vienna in 1670. Although Leopold I treated the Jewish population severely, he had Samson Wertheimer, a Jewish economic adviser who co-operated the banker Samuel Oppenheimer, working for him. They and their families were allowed to remain in Vienna (around 100 people in all). While the Catholic Church condemned the practice of lending money at interest, or 'usury' as it was pejoratively called, they depended on Jews to raise finance for their armies and to help them promote international trade. Jews were forbidden to engage in many professions and the very few who could become bankers and traders had a small opportunity to rise above subsistence living.

Leopold was followed by the Emperor Charles VI who had no male heirs. In 1747, during the reign of Empress Maria Theresa, the Jews of Hungary were taxed for the privilege of remaining in the empire, and were threatened with expulsion if they did not pay. This was called a tolerance tax. They were not allowed to live in certain areas, including Vienna, Pest (Budapest), Croatia or Slovenia. Laws were introduced to allow only the eldest son in a Jewish family to marry in an attempt to reduce the Jewish population. In 1777, Maria Theresa wrote of the Jews: 'I know of no greater plague than this race, which on account of its deceit, usury and avarice is driving my subjects into beggary. Therefore as far as possible, the Jews are to be kept away and avoided.'[1]

In 1780, Joseph II who was influenced by the Enlightenment, succeeded and started working on the assimilation of the Jewish population into Austrian society in order to make them useful to the state. He relaxed some of the restrictions on the Jews in exchange for them enlisting in the army, attending governmental schools where they learnt German and abandoning some of the self-rule they had established in the ghetto. 'Although generally hailed by the upper-class and secularly educated Jews, these edicts were viewed by the vast majority of Jews as sinister attempts to undermine traditional Jewish life.'[2] Many of the restrictions on Jews were reintroduced when Joseph II died. Jewish children were forced to attend Christian schools and only permitted prayers in 'the language of the state'.[3] This mixture of liberalisation and restrictions continued when Francis II, the last Holy Roman Emperor, was defeated by Napoleon at the Battle of Austerlitz and became Francis I, the first Emperor of Austria, ruling from 1804-1835. It was only after the 1848 revolution that the restrictive marriage laws were abolished along with the Jewish Tax. However there were restrictions on civil servant jobs (1851) and Jews were excluded from the possession of land (1853) and from certain professions, such as some legal professions and teaching which affected Wilhelm's father and it was only in 1867 that Jews received full citizenship rights. The period from 1867 to the *Anschluss* in 1938 was merely 71 years and even in this period Jews faced discrimination.

However for those like Wilhelm, growing up after 1867, life seemed truly blessed compared with their parents' generation. The forward-looking Austrian Jews moved over the short period from commerce into industry, and then, into the liberal professions and the arts, in part because of opportunity and in part in order to flee the ghetto stereotype and establish their credentials. This is most vividly described by Stephen Zweig in his autobiography *The World of Yesterday* and in Peter Singer's biography of his grandfather *Pushing Time Away: My Grandfather and the Tragedy of Jewish Vienna*.

Zweig was born in 1881, eight years after Wilhelm Hollitscher. He describes his parents' and grandparents' lives in Moravia (now in the Czech Republic) as peaceful and stable, with good relationships with the country towns and villages where his father sold manufactured goods until he started a textile factory in Bohemia (Western Czech Republic). Unlike the Hollitschers though, Zweig's family were already wealthy and cultured. His mother came from a banking family in Ancona in Italy and his father played the piano and spoke English and French. But he argues that people acquired wealth so they could focus on culture. Vienna, he says, was a city of music and tolerance and you were not truly Viennese without a love of culture. Jews were still locked out of senior positions in the army, politics and the civil service and only had parity in the arts and culture. Vienna had lost its sense of direction and the Jews from the 1880s injected new strength into it. He talks about the peaceful time before the First World War allowing new intellectual thinking. 'I had never loved our old world more than before WW1, I had never hoped more for a united Europe. I had never believed more in its future than at that time when we thought there was a new dawn in sight. But its red hue was really the firelight of the approaching international conflagration.'[4]

Similarly, Peter Singer, writing about his grandfather David Ernst Oppenheim (born 20 April 1881 in Brünn, now Brno) says:

> He came of age at the end of a century of peace and progress. European civilisation was at its peak. Europe ruled the world because it was more enlightened than any other civilisation before it- or so it seemed. For the educated classes in Vienna, life was good. It was not

difficult to earn an income sufficient for a comfortable apartment with a live-in maid, evenings at Vienna's famous opera or theatre, time to sit and chat over an excellent slice of cake at a coffeehouse, and in summer, a vacation by one of Austria's many lakes set amid tranquil forests and alpine peaks.[5]

However this period was not as rosy as Zweig or Singer portrays it. Firstly, life for ordinary Jews moving to Vienna was very tough as Simon Hollitscher testified in his memoir.

Secondly, during this period, Vienna elected an antisemitic Mayor, Karl Lueger, often seen as a forerunner of Nazism. In 1888 he brought together the German National (*Deutschnationale*) and Christian Social factions at City Hall to form a group that later became known as the United Christians (*Vereinigte Christen*). In the 1895 the Christian Social party took political power from the ruling Liberals and paved the way for Lueger to win the mayoralty. The emperor, Franz Joseph, was opposed to the appointment, but after Lueger was elected three consecutive times and the Pope intervened, the emperor was compelled to accept his election. During the period of his authority until his death in 1910, Lueger removed Jews from positions in the city administration and forbade them from working in the factories located in Vienna. Hitler was in Vienna in 1908-1913 and learnt from Lueger. He was rejected by the art and architectural university while many Jews were admitted and this strengthened his antisemitism.

Simon Sebag Montefiore in his 2016 TV programmes on Vienna called it the *City of Ideas* where extremes clashed: Communism versus Fascism; pious formality versus sexual liberation and decadence; monarchy versus revolution. He concludes that while the Habsburgs headed for extinction, Vienna blossomed. As the theories of Freud and the sensuality of the succession artists like Klimt and Schiele ushered in the modern age, Hitler and Stalin stalked[6] the streets. It was here that the First World War was sparked. It was here that Hitler and Stalin dreamt of great Empires which created the Second World War.

Following the First World War, 'Vienna ceased to be the seat of an imperial court ruling over fifty-five million people and instead became the top-heavy capital of a tiny landlocked, mostly alpine republic with a population of less than seven million'.[7] In 1860, the Jewish community in Vienna in numbered 6,200. After the First World War, a total of 200,000 Jews lived in the new, tiny Austria. While in 1919 'Red Vienna', elected a social democratic government that lasted until 1934, Austria remained dominated by the Christian Social party which was strong in rural regions and antisemitic. In 1932 Engelbert Dollfuss, a Christian Social politician, became Chancellor in the midst of a crisis for the conservative government.

By May 1932, Dollfuss[8] began to rule by decree without parliament, outlawed most parties, including the Nazis, and created a right-wing coalition, which he named the 'Fatherland Front', that was committed to independence and the Catholic Church. On 12 February 1934, the Social Democrats used their paramilitary force (*Schutzbund)* to begin an armed attack in an attempt to seize the government and return to a system of democratic rule. But Dollfuss countered by using both the army and his paramilitaries (*Heimwehr).* In the four-day Civil War, 'Red Vienna' was quickly crushed, with violence, which included troops firing artillery into the workers' housing projects. The Social Democrats were defeated and there were many arrests. Constitutional courts were abolished, trade unions and the Social Democrat Party were banned, and the death penalty was reintroduced. Any opposition to Fascism was stamped on and in this context the *Anschluss* took place in 1938. Lisl Hollitscher left Vienna for Egypt by early 1935. Hansl left for England after *Kristallnacht* in November 1938. Their father Wilhelm left for England in March 1939.

Simon Hollitscher (1839-1927)

Wilhelm's father Simon was born in Nikolsburg (Yiddish), now Mikulov, a town in the South Moravian Region of the Czech Republic. It was on the border of Lower Austria from where the Jews had been expelled and on the main road from Vienna (which was 53 miles or 85 kilometers away) to Brünn (now Brno). Therefore, it was an important trading centre and as close to Vienna as Jews were permitted to live. In the first half of the sixteenth century Nikolsburg became the seat of the regional Rabbi of Moravia, thus becoming a cultural centre of Moravian Jewry. By the time of Maria Theresa there were 620 Jewish families in the town comprising roughly half the total population of some 6,000 people.

Simon's grandfather's name was Anschele Narr. In those days every 'ghetto' had its jester whose task it was to amuse society at parties, especially at weddings. Simon says that: 'Anschele was better than most, for you need to be very wise and very clever to be a jester. He lives on in the memory of his community and many a witty word has been attributed to him. The regard in which he was held may be demonstrated by the fact that the local Rabbi at the time, the famous Rabbi Mordechai Benet, himself wrote his epitaph.'[9].

Simon Hollitscher with his granddaughter Lisl, at a holiday house in Austria. The photo was taken by Lisl's brother Hansl when he was around 16 in 1927 © Oppenheimer family

Restriction meant there were few ways for Jews to make a living. One way was to marry a Catholic and avoid these restrictions. Simon's uncle decided to get baptised and married a Catholic girl and then became a doctor. Simon's father, whose name was Jochanan, did not want to take this route so his only option was to become a 'Dorfgeher' (a travelling salesman/peddler). Simon describes his father's work as follows:

> Today's generation find it difficult to imagine a 'Dorfgeher'. The 'Dorfgeher' would leave early on Sunday mornings with his sack on his back carrying only one loaf of home-baked bread and a wooden box containing cheese and dried stock with which to make a soup. And this had to last him for a whole week. It was like this that my father would leave for Aspern an der Zana,[10] eight hours away, whether in hot sunshine or in thick snow in the freezing cold. He would return home on the Sabbath and on feast days to renew his strength among his family – ready to face again the toil and troubles which life held. Now my father was anything but suited to being a

'Dorfgeher'. He preferred to read a good book, especially the Bible and Schopenhauer.

As he concludes: 'It is not hard to imagine that under such circumstances, poverty and misery soon set in.' However Simon argues that, like his father, he was always proud of being Jewish. He relates that, as the small market town of Aspern an der Zana (county Mistelbach) took eight hours to get to, his father sometimes used to spend the Sabbath in Aspern. Simon was once sent to Mistelbach on business on Friday afternoon and wanted to surprise his father at Aspern. 'It was already dark when I got there and I found my father in the inn sitting at a separate table on which the innkeeper had laid a white tablecloth and two Sabbath candles especially for him. It would never have occurred to any of the local guests who were there, out of respect and reverence, to disturb my father's Sabbath day of rest.'

Since Jews were encouraged to attend German-speaking schools, Simon attended the Primary School (eight years) and a lower secondary school (two years) in Nikolsburg. Both were run by the Order of 'Piarists'.[11] He then transferred to Brünn[12] to continue his secondary schooling but he had no money. 'I just managed to survive by having "diet" days, consisting of a midday meal and a loaf of bread which my parents sent me on the Brünn coach once a week, and which I picked up from The Blue Lion inn in Altbrünn. Breakfast and the evening meal consisted of dry bread.' But after the first class of the higher secondary school his 'diet' days got the better of him, and he was forced to give up his studies. He got a job as a 'clerk' in the offices of a Moravian-Silesian county lawyer, Doctor Sigmund Schmelkes. He worked for this man for 25 years until the early1880s. Simon describes him as 'a man of incredible immorality and a tyrannical vulture in the practice of his profession'.

> The Nikolsburg manor, whose owner at that time was the last male offspring of the house of Dietrichstein and who grossly neglected his estate, was taken over by an estate manager called Ratzer. Allotments on the nobleman's grounds were leased to villagers. If lessors failed to make payments when they were due, they – who were without exception well-to-do gentry who possessed little or no land themselves – were passed over to Dr Schmelkes for prosecution. Dr Schmelkes at that time was the only lawyer for miles around. The estate manager and the judge worked closely together to make as much as they could from the villagers. Some poor devil came into the office one day and begged for leniency and deferment of the

amount due but he was seized by the scruff of his neck and thrown out. When such scenes occurred my heart bled and tears crept into my eyes.

When Jews were finally allowed to own property and become lawyers in 1867, five new lawyers established practices in Nikolsburg and others moved into the surrounding area and Dr Schmelkes's practice did less and less well. Simon joined the law firm of Dr Albert Trampusch. His attitude to Albert Trampusch in contrast to Dr Schmelkes tells us much about the liberal environment in which Wilhelm grew up. Simon describes Dr Albert Trampusch as follows:

> He was a tall gaunt figure and so thin, caused by a great deal of suffering, you could almost see his bones. He had deep furrows on his face but such bright and soulful, large blue eyes that shone with goodness and friendliness the like I have never seen in my life. He was well known throughout the town, self-confident and walked with an upright, proud gait. He was an 1848 activist, a Member of the Frankfurt Parliament and was part of the delegation sent from the Parliament to Vienna regarding the release of Blum.[13] There, instead of securing Blum's release, he was taken to the notorious 'Spielberg' where he spent several years as a prisoner.[14] He was given an amnesty later and after a long period of preparation, firstly in the Ministry of Giskra[15], who was also a member of the Frankfurt Parliament at the same time as himself, he became a lawyer. My joining his firm was merely a formality. I was actually working for myself as I transferred all my clients from Dr Schmelkes's firm when it closed. Dr Trampusch never asked me for a management fee even though he hardly had any work and I was fairly busy.

Eventually the work at Dr Trampusch dried up and Simon decided, in around 1887, to go to Vienna to work as a solicitor with his cousin, Dr Friedrich, who only offered him a monthly salary of 60 gulden which is equivalent to 600 Euros a month in 2015.[16] Nikolsburg had ceased to be such an important trading station and since 1848 the number of Jews in the town had been declining. Vienna was the city of opportunity. But Simon was reluctant to desert the graves of his ancestors. Wilhelm recounts in his diary how a few years later, after they were established in Vienna, he visited Nikolsburg with his father and he recalls how his father took leave at the grave of our grandparents in tears: 'he was already over 50 and I felt as if we were being exiled from our homeland, driven away from the graves, I shall never forget that heavy hour'.[17] Wilhelm was going to similarly take leave of two of his siblings' graves when he escaped from Nazi-dominated Vienna.

Simon had left his wife and six children and one foster child in Nikolsburg. He was supporting the children's education and none of the children were yet earning an income. He describes his first year in Vienna as one of terrible suffering. He was living with two extraordinary good nephews – brothers – who charged no rent, and surviving for the most part on water and bread. In this way he could send home his salary almost untouched. He could have received a subsidy from one of his relatives who had earlier converted to Christianity but he 'was simply too proud or, if you like, too stupid'.

Photo of Wilhelm Hollitscher (taken around 1880), on the right, with his mother Blumetta Bertha Betty Hollitscher (née Deutsch), known as Betty Hollitscher. From left to right are: Marie, Jacob (the youngest son, known as Hans after the eldest child who died of meningitis as a baby), Marc, Hanna, Ida sitting on the chair, and Wilhelm our grandfather. Four of Wilhelm's nieces and nephews were killed in the Holocaust and one, who survived, died childless. Two step-daughters of one of his nieces (Anny, who married Karl Winiewicz) did survive. Fritz had not yet been adopted so is not in this photo. He and Wilhelm's eldest sister Hanna also perished in the Holocaust. Black and white photograph, © Oppenheimer family

Simon Hollitscher with grandchildren Lisl and Hansl around 1915, black and white photo, with permission of Susanna von Canon

So Wilhelm was bought up in a liberal observant household. His father was clear that by 'religion' he did not mean the cult: 'I am to a certain extent fairly liberal in these matters – but rather an unshakeable belief in a greater being and neither Darwin nor Häckel[18] can persuade me otherwise.' His family experienced extreme poverty and his father had to work hard to emancipate and educate his children. But the household was large, warm, humorous and lively with all the children bathed in love by their parents.

His father placed a strong emphasis on human kindness describing in his memoir the adoption of Fritz which was done without hesitation despite the poverty of the family.

> There was a man called David Kohn, a bookkeeper whose family lived in the same corridor as ourselves. He and his wife, who were not particularly well-off, died very quickly one after the other in the space of a few weeks, leaving behind five children at a very tender and sensitive age. We, or rather my kind-hearted wife and my daughter Marie, adopted their boy, Friedrich (Fritz). He was treated so much as one of our own children that he hardly felt the loss of his parents at all. He is now a bookkeeper in a reputable wholesalers. He officially changed his name a short time ago to 'Hollitscher' and is an upright good boy. I wish him luck and give him my blessing for his future life as any father would to a child of his own.

All this was to give Wilhelm a firm moral foundation, an ability to deal with hardship, a strong identification with a liberal Judaism, an attachment to family and significant social skills.

Wilhelm's Life

Wilhelm was born 21 February 1873, six years after Jews received full citizenship rights. His father was still working as a lawyer's clerk for Dr Schmelkes and the family were poor. Wilhelm was closest to his sister Marie, whom he called Mitzi. She was two years older than him. She was later to take key responsibility for fostering Fritz and she became a primary school teacher. She never married and died in 1934. He was also very fond of his little sister Ida who was four years younger. The children attended a Jewish Primary School but would have spoken German. Wilhelm was very musical and sang in the synagogue.

Before 1867 there were only ten Czech Gymnasium (equivalent to secondary grammar schools) in the whole of Czechoslovakia, mostly in Bohemia. By 1894 their number had grown to forty one.[19] These widening opportunities enabled lower-middle-class and even some working-class youth to join the modern educated middle classes.[20] In Nikolsburg there was Pearstin Gymnasium which the children attended. This also took students from the small towns and villages in the surrounding area, as well as pupils who had done poorly in the Brünner and Viennese Gymnasium. These pupils lived as lodgers with various families including the

Hollitschers, and their house was the main gathering point of the Jewish students. The income from lodgers supplemented Simon's salary.

When Ida died in June 1942, Wilhelm wrote a eulogy for his sister. This contains the only description of his young adult life.

> In 1886 we moved to Vienna. These were years of struggle for the necessities of life for my parents and naturally also for us children. Mother was not able to withstand the physical and mental stresses. In the third year of our stay in Vienna she was struck by heart trouble. Ida became her carer. Not yet thirteen, she undertook most of the housework. Very early in the morning before she went to school, she had already tidied up, made breakfast, and in the break between morning and afternoon school she prepared lunch, washed up and when she reached home after school at four o'clock, all sorts of tasks were waiting for her. That she found the time to study, to do her homework, so she was always the best behaved and outstanding pupil in her class, is proof of an unusual will-power and sense of duty. Between Ida's sixteenth and twenty-second birthdays, I was away from home. The heart disease of my mother got worse and worse so that she could no longer work but had to be cared for. Ida had to run the house by herself. My elder sister Mitzi, as well as doing her job as a primary school teacher, gave private lessons, so she was out of the house between 7:30 and late evening. It was not an easy task for Ida – she had to cook for ten people, look after mother, look after my small foster brother Fritz – she was always cheerful and up-beat. There was a distinct improvement when I returned to Vienna in 1899. By February 1900, we moved into a larger flat with a bathroom, we took in lodgers, we had a cleaning lady and a washerwoman. The household only consisted of my two sisters, myself and Fritz. My oldest sister was married, my eldest brother was in Goblonz[21] as a 'koncipient'[articled lawyer]. The younger brother was in Switzerland. When my mother's health was tolerable, the house resounded with joy and jollity. It was the central gathering point of a small circle of my sister and my own male and female friends. We played a lot of music, sang, went on excursions together. In 1901, my oldest brother came home, married, and established himself as a lawyer in Vienna. The time of material deprivation was over.

As he explains he was away from home for six years. Some of this time he may have been doing his military service.[21] When his son Hansl was called

Wilhelm Hollitscher around 1908, black and white photograph taken by Eugen Schöfer, Wien, © Oppenheimer

up in the Second World War in the USA, Wilhelm recalled his military service and the Spartan conditions. He described how 40 men shared one room for eating and sleeping, storing their clothes and utensils, washing-up, cleaning and writing. They dug holes for latrines which were emptied by lorries.

But some of the time was also spent completing his Engineering studies in Germany. He commented that 'Austria is more liberal than Germany, where I worked from 1898-99 and where you stepped off the pavement when encountering an officer'. He probably had a job in order to finance his studies. When he returned home in 1899 he worked for Donaudampfschiffahrtsgesellschaft (First Danube Steamboat Shipping Company), founded in 1829 by the Austrian government to transport passengers and cargo on the Danube. By 1880, the DDSG was the world's largest river shipping company. He tells Hansl that when he was a machinist on the Danube (maybe as part of his training), the machine room was 50

This small etching was found with his diary. It presumably shows the cranes he invented with a mythical King Kong type figure in the background.

degrees centigrade and he was on duty from 4am to 9pm with one hour for lunch. He worked hard, often over 60 hours a week. He rose to the position of chief engineer. Lida Winiewicz, Wilhelm's step-niece, relates that he designed four huge cranes for the DDSG at the docks where the steamships arrived. Her father named them 'Onkel Willi's WunderWerke' and the children would laugh and sing out OWIWUWE when they saw those four enormous constructions.

On 31 May 1908 when he was 35, he married Marianne Tedesco who was then aged 23. They had two children, Betti-Lisbeth [Lisl] born in August 1909 and Hans [Hansl] born in August 1911.

He was close friends with both Martin Bunzl (1879-1952) and Paul Tedesco (1872-1923). When he died in 1943 Martin wrote to his daughter Lisl saying: 'It is 45 years ago since I got to know your father and I'm now the last one of the former "clover" (threesome) circle of friends to whom in our youth your father, Paul Tedesco and I belonged.' Martin was to obtain a visa and finance Wilhelm's escape from Vienna and day-to-day living in England from 1939. Paul was Marianne's eldest brother and probably

Wilhelm Hollitscher and Marianne (née Tedesco) probably at the time of their marriage in 1908, black and white photograph, © Oppenheimer

introduced them. Paul and Marianne were Martin's first cousins but were very close since their parents were a brother and sister who married a brother and sister. Wilhelm must have considered himself lucky to marry Marianne. The Tedesco and Bunzl family were more established than the Hollitscher family. The Bunzls had founded a haberdashery business in 1854 and in 1880 moved quickly to set up businesses in Budapest and Vienna purchasing the textile waste that the 'Dorfgehers' often collected to sort and resell for new textiles and paper. Soon they purchased Ignaz Ortmann's rag shedding plant in Pernitz, about 50 miles from Vienna, which was their first venture into manufacturing. Expansions in manufacturing and trading continued in Ortmann, Vienna, Budapest,

Marianne Hollitscher with her son Hansl, early 1912, © Oppenheimer

Zagreb (capital of Croatia) and Teplitz (now Teplice in the Czech Republic). By the First World War the firm had branches in all the countries of the then Austro-Hungarian Empire.So Marianne was comparatively well off and very beautiful. But their marriage was not a happy one.

Wilhelm's love life was complicated and like most of his generation he saw men and women's lives in traditional, gendered roles. That is already clear in his eulogy to Ida where there is no suggestion that he or Fritz could have helped her with the housework. Before he married Marianne, he had an affair with a maid called Pustejovski and she became pregnant and had a daughter called Mimi Pustejovski. Wilhelm acknowledged and supported his daughter. A liaison with a non-Jewish maid would have been frowned upon. It is possible that she died before he married Marianne or more likely he encouraged her to marry someone else but he kept up with his daughter Mimi. She then had two children – Otfried and Else. On 17 August 1939 he says he at last has a postcard from Mimi with photos of her children. On his 67th birthday on the 21 February 1940 he speculates sadly as to whether he will ever see Mimi and her children again. She did survive the war in Vienna despite having a Jewish father, so the lack of formal recognition was helpful in the end.

By 1923 his marriage to Marianne had broken down. She was given to fits of rage and depression. Lisl, aged fourteen, moved out of the family home and went to live with Wilhelm's sister, Ida, who did not have any children. Hansl stayed with his mother. He too was to suffer from depression and had electric shock treatment in 1961. But he always claimed that his mother's mental health issues were exaggerated. Wilhelm remained in the family home but when he fled from Vienna, Marianne did not want to go with him and believed that, as an older woman, she was in no danger. She continued to correspond with Wilhelm and they remained on reasonable terms. Later she was to realise her mistake and her brother Karl, who was in Switzerland, in August 1941 booked her onto a ship from Portugal to the USA, where her son Hansl had arranged a visa. Her last letter to her son Hansl, whom she clearly adored, was written nine days before she was shot on arrival in Kaunas County, Lithuania on 29 November 1941 aged 56. It was carefully worded for the censor and showed that she knew she was being deported.

20/11/1941
Dear Hansl,
I hope that a gentleman with whom I lived in the flat has already reported to you about me but I want to tell you not to worry. I am

relatively well. Who knows when I shall again have the opportunity to write to you, so I am going to do it today myself in any case in order to send you heartiest Christmas wishes. Keep well, dear boy, and don't forget me completely. May the New Year bring you lots of pleasures. I wanted to write to you on the 10th. Unfortunately I was not able to do so. Yesterday I thought of you, in particular, a lot… Probably much will change on Sunday. I find your picture on the photo-slide very good and the receipt of it, as well as your letter, significantly improved my mood…My thoughts will always be with you. Hopefully I shall be hearing from you soon. Unfortunately I won't be able to write often. Who knows how all this will pan out. Don't forget me completely. Please give my love to Lisl too. Hopefully next year things will be better and you, dear boy, keep in good health. Hugs and kisses
Your Mother

Once his marriage collapsed, Wilhelm started a secret affair with Lucie Mehrfeld (L.M.), the daughter of his hairdresser. She lent him 9,500RM (Reichsmark), the money needed for the flight to Bern, when he fled Vienna. Wilhelm had kept a diary from 1914 which he also left with her and also some family heirlooms, but we have been unable to trace any of this. Lucie lived in Wien 111, Disslergasse 1 in a pleasant street just across the canal from what was then – and is still today – the Jewish quarter, Leopoldstadt. Wilhelm says in his diary that Lucie was 'honest and good'. In August 1939 he writes: 'A letter from L. M. I miss her very much. Will I see her ever see her again, kiss her one more time in my life? She writes she wants to see me one more time, then she would die peacefully'. As he sits in his room in September 1939 he reflects: 'There are so many I have to think of, L.M. in particular?' He refers to her in the diary as L.M., still trying to keep the affair secret and his daughter Lisl did not know about it until after his death. But his sister Ida and his best friend Richard Kann[22] did know her. On the 29 December 1939 he writes: 'Ida spent the afternoon at L.M.'s – was in tears, handed over her old family letters to be kept. I wonder if I shall ever see her again, as God wills.' Early the next year (12/01/40) he says he received a postcard from Leo Kann, Richard's brother, who wrote that 'L.M. was at Richard's (Kann), it is not a secret anymore, just as well!!' She never married and was brave to keep up her contacts with Jewish families into 1940. She was clearly very attached to Wilhelm.

There is little documentary evidence about his life between 1928 and 1935 when he started to write regularly to his daughter in Alexandria, Egypt.

Later letters, however, make it clear that his health deteriorated during this period. In 1928 (aged 55) Wilhelm had a serious illness and major operation (not fully successful), which left him with bladder problems and unable to drink alcohol. In November 1936 he talks about problems with his bladder and prostate. In 1937 he talks again about having prostrate troubles, and thinks his former operation was too early and allowed the prostrate problem to grow again. He was having radiation but it was not as unpleasant as the previous time. Whether it was because of ill health is unclear, but by 1933 he was no longer working for the Donau Steamboat Company and had set up his own business marketing boilers and was struggling to make a modest living. In 1933, he was in Budapest about a licence/patent at Ganz and Co. In 1935 he was trying to obtain a patent with the Simmeringer Masch. Fabr. AG. He provided a giant boiler for the Hohenauer sugar factory. In November 1936 he was the expert witness in a case in Döbling about a motor boat going too fast and nearly drowning swimmers at the Kuchelau bathing pool. His expertise continued to be used until his death and he gave advice to one of the Bunzl factories in England.

There are many parallels with our own times in 1930s Vienna. Instead of the gradual progress towards a greater prosperity and tolerance in society that people expected after the First World War, the depression bought increasing insecurity. Wilhelm's increasing financial insecurity was compounded by the growing antisemitism and the rise of the far right.

Wilhelm would have been particularly concerned about his children. Lisl, who was independently minded, had left Vienna in August 1928 to do a holiday course in French at the University of Nancy. In autumn 1928, aged nineteen, she stayed with a family in Saltash, Cornwall looking after their two little girls as a 'governess'. She then spent the spring term in rural Lincolnshire at a school with thirty pupils aged five to thirteen teaching them French and German, algebra, geometry, drawing, painting and gymnastics. In the summer term she went to the Elliott School in Putney. She returned to Vienna in the summer 1929 to start her law degree at the University of Vienna in the autumn. However, 1930 saw antisemitic riots in the University[23] and it would not have been a welcoming atmosphere. By 1932 Dollfuss was in power, Hitler came to power in Germany in 1933 and 'red Vienna' was smashed in 1934. Lisl started taking practical courses in gymnastics and beauty and cosmetics from September 1933. She also spent periods of time in Egypt writing articles for Viennese newspapers. So as the situation became more uncertain, she widened her opportunities to earn a living and travel to other countries. By April 1935 she had decided to emigrate to Egypt but was clearly homesick and worried about getting an income at first. Wilhelm advised her to be patient. He said that as long as she made enough to pay for a roof over her head, food and clothing and occasional pleasurable activities, she was far better off than in Austria, particularly in comparison with Austrian Jews.

Meanwhile Hansl was just eighteen at the start of the Great Depression. In 1931 there was the collapse of Vienna's two great Rothschild banks, the Bodencredit and the Creditanstalt and growing unemployment. This boosted the Austrian Nazi party, leading both Dollfuss and Schuschnigg to compete for the support of antisemites.[24] Hansl was twenty when Dolfuss became the Chancellor and struggled to get a job. The economic policy of the Austro-fascist regime continued that of earlier governments, under which a balanced state budget and 'sound money' were considered sacrosanct and interest rates were kept high. This 'austerity' had particularly disastrous effects on employment, wages and social progress.[25] Wilhelm's younger brother, Hans Jacob Hollitscher, was involved in the attempt by the small town of Wörgl to print their own currency and run a local 'New Deal' which was very successful but outlawed by the Austrian government. Hans Jacob Hollitscher was later to argue in his major book[26] that the state's insistence on orthodoxy brought about the downfall of Austria with the delivery of the country to the Nazis. It took until November 1936 for Hansl to get his first proper job as a bookkeeper with the company Vacuum. This coincided with Lisl finally getting her law degree and Wilhelm wrote to her in Egypt saying that he and other relations were celebrating the success of both children.

In response to the uncertain political and economic situations and to escape from the problems they faced, Jews tended to turn away from the public sphere to focus on the private.[27] Wilhelm's letters tell of visits to relatives, classes he attended on various topics, his singing activities and summer vacations in the mountains. He was extremely musical and was Vice President of the Vienna Singing Academy, a mixed choir founded in 1858 and conducted by Brahms in 1863. Wilhelm wrote an article on the Vienna Singing Academy which was published in April 1933.[28] Books were an integral part of his life. He read widely, mainly fiction, but also books on philosophy, history, religion, and scientific and technical subjects. Reading was to be his route to learning English.

But his worsening health and events in Austria meant that the political situation could not be ignored for long. A thrombosis in his leg was operated on in February 1938 and he spent 52 days in hospital. While he was there, on 12 March 1938, Germany's 8th Army marched into and annexed the Republic of Austria in the *Anschluss* (Annexation). Many Jews had already tried to escape to Prague but were pulled off the train. In his book, *The Hare with Amber Eyes*, Edmund de Waal[29] vividly describes this first day, when some Austrian Nazis broke into his great grandparents' (the Ephrussi family) house destroying furniture, looting and intimidating his great grandparents. The following day there were arrests of anyone who had supported any previous political party, prominent journalists, financiers, civil servants and Jews. Two days after the *Anschluss*, Hitler arrived in Vienna and the Wehrmacht paraded around the Ring.[30] The Cardinal of Vienna ordered the bells of Austria to chime. The following day 200,000 people jammed into the Heldenplatz (the Heroes' Square) to hear Hitler's speech.

Within months of the *Anschluss*, all Jews were ordered to move to Vienna, and then eventually to the 2nd district (Leopoldstadt). Jews were ordered to change their name to Sara or Israel and wear the Star of David. It was in this atmosphere that Lisl visited him from Egypt with baby Hannah, his first grandchild. They nearly didn't make it back to Alexandria.

For 24 hours from the night of November 8-9, 1938 there were violent riots, wild arrests, and the burning of synagogues and Jewish prayer houses (known as *Kristallnacht* – or 'the night of broken glass'). 680 Jews committed suicide in Vienna, 27 were murdered. Some Jews were sent to the Austrian concentration camp Mauthausen. Others were sent to firms and construction sites as forced labourers. The diary contains Wilhelm's description of this day and how he watched the SS burn down his local synagogue and had the presence of mind not to go home or hang around, but to go to the dentist.

Hansl was determined to emigrate and soon left for Salford, near Manchester, where he prepared for his father to arrive by renting a room and getting a job as a paint sprayer in a factory. Wilhelm was able to follow in March 1939 because his good friend Martin Bunzl had secured visas for all the extended family. The Bunzls had created a parent company in Zug in Switzerland, called Bunzl-Konzern Holdings A.G. (BKH) in 1936, thereby ensuring that their assets could not be expropriated by the Nazis. A company was also created in the UK (Bunzl & Biach (British) Ltd) in 1936 and several factories opened. By 1954 there was a sorting plant at Nottingham, a factory producing cigarette filters in Jarrow, a paper-converting mill also at Jarrow and a Shoddy (the recycling of woollen rags by tearing them up into a material, the Shoddy, which could be processed to make new cloth) factory in Dewsbury, Yorkshire. This effectively saved the lives of both Hansl and Wilhelm and enabled them to establish themselves in England.

In his diary, Wilhelm speaks of his relief, 'like a salvation from a serious illness', as he flew over the Dutch-German border. But arriving as a refugee in Salford was not easy. His English was poor and apart from his son, he was separated from his close friends and relatives and very isolated. The fact that it took two and a half months to re-start the diary, which he had been writing daily for 25 years, evidences his depression once the initial elation of escape had worn off. And the diary makes clear his continual worry about those left behind. In particular, he was anxious about his sister Ida and her husband Gustav who were meant to join him in England but left it too late. They left Vienna in November 1940 and were then lucky to depart for Palestine, sailing from Trieste on 2 December 1939. He was also worried about his friend Richard Kann who left even later, only setting sail on the 21 March 1940 to go from Genoa to the USA. Others, such as his eldest sister Hana and daughter Stella, did not make it, despite his attempts to find Stella a position as a domestic servant in order in bring her to England. But Wilhelm was a positive and resilient person as we see again and again in the diary. His message to himself in Huyton to 'Keep smiling' was part of maintaining a positive response. Through his son he made friends with a group of young refugees aged 17 to 30 and was clearly fully accepted by them. He was to meet one of them again, Otto Hirschhorn, at Huyton.

After Hansl left for the USA, Wilhelm's life was significantly improved by the move to Petts Wood, near Bromley in Northern Kent, now a London suburb. Here he could walk to visit Martin Bunzl and the group of relatives that Martin had helped to move to England. He could get the train up to London to visit more relatives. He could also walk into the countryside and nature meant a lot to him: on his long daily walks he described a flower, bird, butterfly, mushrooms and the changes in the weather. According to Martin Bunzl, he often said that he had been very happy in Petts Wood in his last few years, despite regretting his fate.

The diary reveals a sociable and fun loving man who became a central figure for a group of Austrian detainees in Huyton. He was a good conversationalist and spent time with his friends, fully engaged in discussing the issues of the day and cultural and philosophical questions. He was a 'bon viveur' and food and company were essential to him. Despite being an observant Jew who maintained the Sabbath and celebrated the high holy days, he celebrates the packages which arrive from his Petts Wood relatives: non-Kosher sausages, bacon and Linzer torte (an Austrian tart with a lattice design on top of the pastry made with nuts). All refugees find the food of their childhood and community very comforting. He was deeply religious, but in a spiritual way like his father, rather than a rigid rule follower. In 1942 he went with Dachinger's father to the temple for Passover and said: 'for me it was three and a half hours of devotion which seem to pass in no time'.[31] His philosophy was simple:

> In my opinion every true believer – i.e. people who live passionately and committed with complete honesty according to their convictions – leads a good life. Whatever life events they encounter, their material life will no doubt be driven by circumstances but their internal life will not be changed.[32]

His attitude to German nationalism is interesting. While still in Salford in September 1939 he states: 'I am reading with great pleasure, for the second time Schneider's *Arthur Schopenhauer*, the most significant modern philosopher who has no time for German nationalism and calls the Germans 'the most stupid people'.[33] But he also honestly confides in his diary:

> I often think to myself if I was not a Jew and if Hitler had not made his racial persecution a central plank of his programme, would I have followed him with great enthusiasm? The thought of a future German world power has always attracted me. How depressed I was, when we Austrians were forbidden, after the end of the 1918 war, to join in union with Germany? If I recollect the conversations with Edi Wibbe, how I the Jew supported, and he the German Ayrian opposed, the Germans. How much I mistook their characteristics.[34] (Diary 03/04/40)

This is a reflection of the identity crisis that characterised Austria in the inter-war period. The Austro-Hungarian Empire was not a nation state like Germany and its inhabitants had divided loyalties. Wilhelm grew up in German-speaking Moravia, which was to become Czechoslovakia. He identified culturally with Austria and Germany rather than with a Czech-speaking Slav country. One of his complaints during internment was that Czechs, whom he saw as antisemitic as Austrians, had been treated as allies and victims and had not been interned. But he also had a Jewish identity. The new small Austria that was created after the First World War was far less tolerant of divided loyalties and the Austrians saw themselves as ethnic Germans. Austrian Jews who claimed their Jewish ethnic identity were increasingly scorned as the new republic demanded the unity of political, national, cultural and ethnic loyalty.[35] Wilhelm's reflections quoted above illustrate these tensions.

The experience of the camp must have been horrific for those who had fled Nazi Germany or Austria, just as current internment is an inhuman way to treat asylum seekers from countries like Afghanistan and Iraq. Dachinger's pictures focus on the barbed wire and the feeling of powerlessness and containment. The conditions were particularly bad at the beginning in the early days of chaos when food was not sufficient, there was no toilet paper and discipline was harsh, with warnings that they could be shot if they wondered around at night. Then the internees heard about how the *Arandora Star* was torpedoed just as they were being asked to volunteer to go to Canada and Australia. When there were insufficient volunteers, men were marched at gun point to be deported.

Even the very pro-British author and artist Alfred Lomnitz was to protest. The march from the railway station to Huyton Internment Camp was, he argued, a hard journey mentally not physically.

> They went right through that little town, exposed to all the people. PRISONERS – supposed to be dangerous enemies of the country. ENEMIES – most of them only too anxious to help the people of this country to put an end to this country's enemy – who was their enemy too...[36]

Their first dinner 'consisted of highly bitter tea (one mugful); two slices of white bread; half a square inch of margarine; two square inches of cheddar cheese; and one spoonful of jam. A totally inadequate meal for men who for the last twenty-four hours had been nourished on the shortest travelling rations.'[37] Then a few days later they did not have sufficient volunteers for the ship transport so the Captain just chose people. On the day of the transport, Lomnitz describes a sight he had tried to avoid seeing:

> That grim column of captives trudging through mud at the exit of the Camp with soldiers posted all along the street, their bayonets fixed. A few last shouts of farewell, and the Camp was emptier by 1494 men – six short of the required number. Two had died during the night; two were ill; two refused to go.[38]

Life did get better after the 15 July when the original Commandant of the camp was replaced by Lt. Col. Slatter and Wilhelm's diary does not dwell on the hardships but focusses instead on the positives and the humour he found in adversity. Yet the strain he was under is clear when he admits to bursting into tears on hearing he was going to be released (22 August). 'Suddenly I recognised my own and everyone's misery, the whole charade of jolliness which I act when people are around, collapsed suddenly and I stood there naked.'

When he reflects on his experience in the epilogue he starts by seeing the whole internment policy as a sign of antisemitism and Fascism supported by a faction of the governing classes. There were certainly strong antisemitic elements in the governing classes beyond Ramsay and Mosely (whose arrests he reports on 13 June 1940), who wanted to make a deal with Hitler before and after France fell. Such people called for refugees to be classified as 'enemy aliens' and generated scare-mongering rumours about such aliens being the enemy within. François Lafitte, a social policy analyst, who wrote a famous book on internment in 1940, argued: 'Interning anti-Nazi refugees does not mean security. Security is achieved by interning *"suspects"* whether English or "alien".'[39] He concluded: 'The British government has declared war on the wrong people' and 'its policy of internment and deportation is needlessly discouraging vital progressive forces all over Europe and, maybe, turning friends into enemies'.[40]

However accurate this critique is, what is noticeable about Wilhelm is his lack of bitterness about his internment and how he sees the good side of what he experienced. The one adjective that best describes him is 'kind-hearted'. His decency, altruism and modesty shine through his diary – everyone who met him, liked him. He has an amazing ability to keep up with a very large number of friends and acquaintances, his loyalty and helpfulness to the inner circle of his friends and relatives are striking.

He was also brave and anxious to do good. During the war he was on fire watch duty doing three hours duty every ten days, often in the middle of the night. He returned from the internment camp in the middle of the Blitz. He says in September 1940 that he has been at 14 Crossway, in Petts Wood for 25 days and has experienced 94 air raids, usually from 8p.m. to 5-6a.m. He moved to the ground floor to sleep. Uncle Gustav (who was the half-brother of Martin Bunzl) was not well enough to be moved to the Anderson shelter; he was suffering from stomach cancer. So Wilhelm slept with him. Uncle Gustav finally died on 31 December 1941 and Wilhelm had faithfully visited him every day at 9:30a.m. for the last three months and almost every day before then from January 1940 when he moved to Petts Wood except for the period of his internment.

Ultimately family was the most important part of his life. He wrote to his son and daughter and his siblings at least once a week. Letter-writing was part of his daily routine and why he found the lack of letters in the camp the hardest thing to bear. In writing his diaries his aim was to leave himself to his children, their children and their children's children as a 'human being'. It is his continual sadness that he cannot see his immediate family and his grandchildren that I find most moving in his letters and diary. We are very lucky to have his diary and letters now and understand his legacy of true humanity. It is appropriate to finish this short biography with an extract from the letter that Martin Bunzl sent to my mother Lisl shortly after his death.

Wilhelm Hollitscher with his landlord's dog Todge, June 13 1943, black and white photograph, © Oppenheimer family

I confirm the sad telegram that I had to send you last Friday and which, no doubt, you have now received. Not only you, but we too unfortunately have suffered a great loss through the death of your dear father, who was such a good friend to us and who, through his attitude to life, his joie-de-vivre but also his knowledge, succeeded in enhancing the last few years and making them more bearable. We are all going to miss him dreadfully. You already know how much he doted on you children. He waited with baited breath for each and every letter. He showed us each letter and was proud of his children and grandchildren. When he sensed that he was dying, he began to pray for you. He asked for your photographs and began to kiss them. That says it all...With his passing we have lost a quite special person. You don't often find this synthesis of an affirmative attitude to life and earthly enjoyments linked to a high intellectuality and musicality. And, in addition, his sound philosophy of life, whereby he confronted everything that fate had meted out to him with optimism.

Notes

1 https://mariateresacalderonlomeli.wordpress.com/absolute-power/
2 P. R. Mendes-Flohr, J. Reinharz (eds),*The Jew in the Modern World: A Documentary History* (Oxford: Oxford University Press, 1995), p. 40.
3 https://www.bh.org.il/jewish-spotlight/austria/modern-era/history/until-1867/
4 S. Zweig, *The World of Yesterday* (London: Pushkin Press, 2009), p. 215.
5 P. Singer, *Pushing Time Away: My Grandfather and the Tragedy of Jewish Vienna* (New York: Ecco, 2003), p.10.
6 Soviet dictator Joseph Stalin spent a month in the city in 1913, meeting Trotsky and writing *Marxism and the National Question*, with Nikolay Bukharin, A Walker, *1913: When Hitler, Trotsky, Tito, Freud and Stalin all lived in the same place* (BBC, 18 April 2013 https://www.bbc.co.uk/news/magazine-21859771).
7 P. Singer, *Pushing Time Away*, p.129.
8 An antisemite, Dollfuss had been instrumental in excluding from membership all students 'tainted with Jewish blood' at a Catholic students' congress in 1920. During his chancellorship a number of covert anti-Jewish measures were introduced, and after the crushing defeat of the Social Democrats in February 1934 he refused to see a Jewish delegation, remarking that the Jews should be pleased that he was too busy to deal with Jewish affairs. However, Austrian Jewry regarded him as a 'bulwark against persecution and the horrors of a Nazi regime' (*JC*, July 27, 1934) because of his energetic stand against Nazism. https://www.encyclopedia.com/religion/encyclopedias-almanacs-transcripts-and-maps/dollfuss-engelbertdeg
9 Mordecai ben Abraham Benet (also known as Marcus Benedict), 1753-1829 was a Talmudist and Chief Rabbi of Moravia.
10 This probably refers to Asparn an der Zana, the location of Mamuz castle.

11   Founded by Saint Joseph Calasanctius, the Piarist fathers' aim is to provide free education for poor children.

12   Probably around 1855.

13   Albert Trampusch (1816-1898) was, as Simon states, a member of the Frankfurt National Assembly, which was the first freely-elected parliament (on 1 May 1848) for the whole of Germany. It followed the March 1948 Revolution, and the Frankfurt Constitution proclaimed a German Empire based on the principles of parliamentary democracy. In October a rising in Vienna forced the government to flee, but it then violently suppressed the rising and arrested the deputy, Robert Blum. He was a German democratic politician, publicist, poet, publisher, revolutionary and member of the National Assembly. He was court-martialed and executed, despite his parliamentary immunity. Without the support of Austria or Prussia the Franfurt National Assembly failed.

14   Špilberk Castle (German: Spielberg) is a castle on the hilltop in Brno. Its construction began in the first half of the thirteenth century and it was completed by King Ottokar of Bohemia (1253-78). It was gradually turned from a royal castle into a huge baroque fortress, and was considered the harshest prison in the Empire.

15   Carl Giskra (1820-1879) was from Moravia and was Interior Minister from 1867-1870.

16   https://www.historicalstatistics.org/Currencyconverter.html

17   W. Hollitscher, *Diary*, 13 June 1939.

18   Darwin's 1859 book *On the Origin of Species* had immense popular influence, but although its sales exceeded its publisher's hopes it was a technical book rather than a work of popular science: long, difficult and with few illustrations. One of Haeckel's books did a great deal to explain his version of 'Darwinism' to the world. It was a bestselling, provocatively illustrated book in German, titled *Natürliche Schöpfungsgeschichte*, published in Berlin in 1868, and translated into English as *The History of Creation* in 1876. It was frequently reprinted until 1926.

19   J. Pánek, and O Tůma, *A History of the Czech Lands* (Prague: Charles University, Karolinum Press, 2nd edition 2018), p.377.

20   G.B. Cohen, *Education and Middle-Class Society in Imperial Austria: 1848-1918* (USA, Purdue University Press, 1996).

21   After the creation of the Austro-Hungarian Empire in 1867, a new army law decreed universal three-year conscription followed by a ten-year reserve obligation. In practice, only about one in five of those liable to service were called up, and many were sent on leave after two years.

22   Richard Kann (1874-1944) was Wilhelm's third cousin and best friend. He was one of the last of Wilhelm's friends to leave Vienna only getting to New York in March 1940 and joining his elder brother, Leo, there. His brother Leo was the father of Professor Robert A. Kann who taught at the faculty of the History Department at Rutgers University. Robert Kann devoted himself to the study and teaching of Austrian history, with a particular interest in examining forces of conflict, division, reconciliation and integration. In 1976 he returned to Austria as visiting professor at the University of Vienna and was appointed Honorary Professor of Modern History just before his death in 1981.

23   Hans Neurath, *Being Jewish in Vienna*, Department of Germanics, University of Washington.https://germanics.washington.edu/being-jewish-vienna

24   B. F. Pauley, 'Political Antisemitism in Interwar Vienna', in H. Strauss and W. Bergmann (eds),*Current Research on Antisemitism, Vol 3/2 Hostages of Modernization* (Berlin, New York: Walter de Gruyter, 1993).

25   Gerhard Senft, 'Economic Development and Economic Policies in the Städestaat Era' in G. Bischof, A. Pelinka, A. Lassner (eds), *The Dollfuss/Schuschnigg Era in Austria: A Reassessment*, (New Jersey: Transaction Publishers, 2003), p.44.

26   Erich Hans Wolf (pseudonym of Hans Jacob Hollitscher) *Kastrophenwirtschaft.Gerburt und Ende Österreichs 1918 bis 1938* (Zürich: Europa Verlag, 1939).

27   Hans Neurath, *Being Jewish in Vienna*, https://germanics.washington.edu/being-jewish-vienna

28   Wilhelm Hollitscher, Vice President of the Vienna Singing Academy, 'The Singing Academy Celebrates', *Neues Wiener Tagblatt*, 7 April 1933.

29   E. de Waal, *The Hare with Amber Eyes. A Hidden Inheritance* (Godalming, Surrey, Vintage, 2011).

30   The Ring is a wide tree-lined boulevard that encircles the centre of the city.

31   Wilhelm Hollitscher, letter to Lisl Oppenheimer, 3 April 1942.

32   Wilhelm Hollitscher, *Diary,* 13 August 1940.

33   Wilhelm's grandfather, a peddler ('Dorfgeher'), did not enjoy his job and preferred books, the Bible and Schopenhauer. So the interest in Schopenhauer (1788-1860) comes through his family. Schopenhauer contended that at its core, the universe is not a rational place. He suggested that to overcome a frustration-filled and fundamentally painful human condition we ought to minimize our natural desires and concentrate on artistic, moral and ascetic forms of awareness. Schopenhauer emphasised compassion, which he saw as learnt knowledge, with the good man understanding the suffering of others and not only avoiding harming others, but actively trying to alleviate the suffering of others. (Robert Wicks, *Arthur Schopenhauer,* Stanford Encyclopedia of Philosophy, 2003, revised 2017, https://plato.stanford.edu/entries/schopenhauer/). It was these aspects of Schopenhauer that were probably attractive to Wilhelm. But as he says later (22/09/1939) Schopenhauer was also highly critical of Jewish theology and, although he criticised the treatment of Jews, his writings were coloured by and helped to foster antisemitic trends in German cultural and political life.

34   Wilhelm Hollitscher, *Diary*, 03/04/40

35   Hans Neurath, *Being Jewish in Vienna*, https://germanics.washington.edu/being-jewish-vienna

36   A. Lomnitz, *Never Mind, Mr. Lom: Or the Uses of Adversity* (London: Macmillan and Co. Ltd, 1940), p. 34.

37   Ibid., p.42.

38   Ibid., p.77.

39   F. Lafitte, *The Internment of Aliens* (London: Libris 1940, 1988), p. 210.

40   Ibid., p.253.

e 1: *Female Nude with Red Vase*, Hugo Dachinger, 1940, watercolour and gouache on wallpaper, National
eums Liverpool, Walker Art Gallery, © The Estate of Hugo Dachinger, Photograph courtesy of National
eums Liverpool.

Plate 2A: *Waiting Waiting…*, Hugo Dachinger, 1940, watercolour on paper, National Museums Liverpool, Walker Art Gallery, © The Estate of Hugo Dachinger, Photograph courtesy of National Museums Liverpool.

Plate 2B: *Potato Peelers*, Hugo Dachinger, 1940, crayon, watercolour and gouache on paper, National Museums Liverpool, Walker Art Gallery, © The Estate of Hugo Dachinger, Photograph courtesy of National Museums Liverpool.

Plate 3: *Portrait of a Man in Blue Sweater and Brown Jacket, His Right Hand Raised to his Head*, Hugo Dachinger, 1940, watercolour and gouache on wallpaper, National Museums Liverpool, Walker Art Gallery, © The Estate of Hugo Dachinger, Photograph courtesy of National Museums Liverpool.

Plate 4: *Two Internees Bowing in Front of an Officer*, Hugo Dachinger, 1940, pen, ink and watercolour on pap
National Museums Liverpool, Walker Art Gallery, © The Estate of Hugo Dachinger, Photograph courtesy
National Museums Liverpool.

Plate 5: *Portrait of a Man Wearing Blue Shirt and Red Tie*, Hugo Dachinger, 1940, gouache on newspaper, National Museums Liverpool, Walker Art Gallery, © The Estate of Hugo Dachinger, Photograph courtesy of National Museums Liverpool.

Plate 6: *Dinner in Campton Park: Vitamins Enlisted to Win the War*, Hugo Dachinger, 1940, watercolour and gouache on newspaper, National Museums Liverpool, Walker Art Gallery, © The Estate of Hugo Dachinger, Photograph courtesy of National Museums Liverpool.

Plate 7: *Identity Lost*, Hugo Dachinger, 1940, pastel, watercolour and gouache on newspaper, National Museums Liverpool, Walker Art Gallery, © The Estate of Hugo Dachinger, Photograph courtesy of National Museums Liverpool.

Plate 8A: *Dead End*, Hugo Dachinger, 1940, watercolour and gouache on newspaper and canvas, National Museums Liverpool, Walker Art Gallery, © The Estate of Hugo Dachinger, Photograph courtesy of National Museums Liverpool.

Plate 8B: *Perimeter Fence Under Red Sky*, Hugo Dachinger, 1940, watercolour and gouache on newspaper, National Museums Liverpool, Walker Art Gallery, © The Estate of Hugo Dachinger, Photograph courtesy of National Museums Liverpool.

4

Wilhelm Hollitscher's Huyton Diary

England, Salford, 13 June 1939

I would like to try and start with my diary entries again. In the last few months, during my Vienna stay, I kept my notes irregularly.

My memory is not reliable anymore; it means that my notes written from memory are not very reliable. I left Vienna on 29 March at 10.30. The last weeks before emigration were agonising: the days full with running around, errands, shopping, farewell visits, and the actual absurdity of the 'bustling activity' ruined my nerves – continuous heart complaints, dizziness and headaches. My few savings are completely gone.

Particular events before my departure: on 26 March, Saturday, I went to the cemetery with Ida [sister],[1] took leave of the graves of our parents and of Marc's [brother][2] and Mini's [sister][3] graves. I remember how I visited Nikolsburg[4] with my father and how he took leave at the grave of our grandparents in tears – he was already over 50 and I felt as if we were being exiled from our homeland, driven away from the graves, I shall never forget that heavy hour. Gustidl [Gustav and Ida] accompanied me to the airport: Gustav [brother-in-law][5] was led off for a body search during which the officials stole eighty Reichmarks out of his wallet. An example of the state theft which has spread to the very lowest circles.

The feeling, when I sat in the Dutch airplane, when I flew over the German-Dutch border, was like a salvation from a serious illness.

In London I saw everyone. In Manchester, Hansl [son][6] expected me; first impression, obviously influenced by the miserable weather, depressing. Flat: English detached house, Salford (connected to Manchester), Jewish, elegant residential area, a nice room which I share with Hansl, the most beautiful basin with hot and cold running water, a young couple, two young boys (4 years and 7 months). Because of the lack of language skills I'm very lonely, try to learn, depressed, cannot memorise, miserable pronunciation. I live like a recluse.

Spain, thanks to Italian and German help, has settled the war in favour of Franco's dictatorship – it is 'desolating' and I sit here, in a different part of the world – apathetic and resigned – wait, wait, wait, what for?...That God grants me some luck, to live a few years peacefully and to live to see the happiness of my children and those who are close to me.

1 September 1939

The world will make a note of this 1 September. Yesterday evening, the German broadcasting station published sixteen points, which Poland had to accept by 8 o'clock last night. Hitler demanded, without any notification beforehand, that Poland should send a representative to Berlin, who would be authorised to sign. As Poland hasn't sent anybody, Hitler (= Germany) considers that his 'peaceful' demands have been declined. As a result, an army call up and, according to the latest reports tonight, bombardments on Rybnik and another two cities; a war without a war declaration.

2 o'clock in the afternoon.

The war has started and German troops crossed the Polish borders, German bombers bombarded Rybnik, Katowice, Krakow, Warsaw, Vilnius. Hitler spoke at the Reichstag, lied to perfection, said the Western powers are to blame, he thanked Stalin for his support, but declared that he will battle it out on his own...England will fulfil its duty. Parliament is convened for tonight. France proclaimed martial law.

For me, thinking about events at the beginning of the war, the biggest sensation is to observe how the population accepts events with a stiff upper lip – one can almost say with composure. It seems as if everybody regards it as a matter of fact, as their duty, if you can regard it as one. All safety measures are carried out in a quiet and calm way. Despite evacuation etc. daily life is untouched, business as usual.

I am frightened, a vague anxiety, based on the knowledge that two fanatics like Hitler and Stalin have got the power to do whatever they see fit.

3 September 1939

This morning at 11 o'clock Prime Minister Chamberlain announced the war with Germany...Immediately after Chamberlain's statement it was announced on the radio that all public amusement places, theatre, cinema etc. have been closed. Everybody should carry a gas mask when going out. Air raid warning signals were made known etc. And now I am waiting for the (new) regulations for the refugees and the way it will happen.

4 September 1939

Yesterday at 5pm France declared war on Germany. At 6 pm the King held his radio broadcast. He must have been very nervous, because his speech impediment – stutter – was very noticeable. At 8pm the Archbishop of Canterbury spoke, apparently false war reports from both sides. The refugees have to report and bring their documents. Further action is not yet thought through. We (the refugees) are only allowed to move within five miles from home – fair enough!

5 September 1939

Yesterday, Hansl and I reported to the main police station in due form. A note was affixed on our certificate of registration with conduct instructions. We are 'alien enemy'; however they intend to find ways to treat all refugees in the same way. The Czech refugees are not considered as 'enemy'. Everything is continuing to be calm.

25 September 1939

The day before yesterday was Yom Kippur, the Day of Atonement. The previous evening and yesterday morning I was in the Temple and had been honestly fasting for a while. Yom Kippur started with the Kol Nidrei, the controversial, extraordinary prayer (going back to the seventh century) which resulted in so much persecution and suffering for the Jews and which is malignly interpreted by the enemies of the Jews. This prayer specifically says that God releases them from all debt, oaths and duties which they have committed to in the previous year, whether they have committed to binding duties and oaths or are non-believers. Are confession and absolution rooted in this or has this prayer arisen from them? The thought that on this evening in the whole world, where Jews are scattered – living as members of different people and nations – this 'national prayer' of the Jews is sung with the same passion and age-old melody first used 1,200 years ago, is overwhelming and gives me the hope that this exemplary traditional tenacity and admirable faith of the Jews who are believers will succeed in overcoming all storms. My prayer was that God should grant my wish to end my days in my homeland and be buried in the grave of my parents and Mimi and Marc.

27 September 1939

Yesterday Chamberlain and Churchill spoke in Parliament. The radio war is part of the most interesting aspect of the war; every state broadcasts its 'lies' across the world, in all manner of significant languages. From here there are broadcasts in: German, French, Italian, Czech, Polish, Hungarian, Swedish, Norwegian, Danish, Spanish, Portuguese, Arabic, Serb, Romanian, and I believe also in Indian. In their German broadcasts the English have discovered a good trick; they use recordings of former speeches from one or two years or a few months ago and compare them with the current facts – nothing has remained of Hitler's world view, only the Jewish question has been pursued totally.

30 September 1939

Well, Russia and Germany have signed an agreement. Poland is finally going to be carved up; Germany gets the bigger portion, Russia pulls back from the boundaries of territories which it has temporarily occupied. Warsaw and Lublin are to be handed to the Germans, intervention of a third party is forbidden.

Now that the Polish question has been settled there seem to be no grounds for continuing the war between Germany and the Allies, Hitler will offer a peace proposal. If it is not accepted, Germany and Russia will discuss further policy. Russia will furnish Germany with war materials in return for manufactured products. Those people that fall under German rule will be governed by the Nazi (Hitler) regime; those in Russia by a Bolshevik regime. At the same time a treaty between Russia and Estonia has been made public, the latter becomes a Russian vassal state. Despite the assurance of England and France that this treaty does not change anything and that war will continue, the fact of the coming together of Russia and Germany amounts, in my opinion, to a defeat of the Western powers.

12 October 1939

Important personal matters. Hansl has to appear at the American Consulate on 24 October to receive his American visa. The question of whether he is going to emigrate or stay here has to be thoroughly deliberated. And I? Alone.

10 November 1939

Today is the one-year anniversary of the pogrom in Germany. As long as I live I shall never forget how, as I walked onto the road and took a few steps towards the synagogue, I suddenly heard heavy gunfire. I saw two men on the external staircase that provides access to the women's area. I watched how they smashed the windows, threw bombs into the synagogue, ran down the steps again, spoke with two guards, got into their car driven by a SS man and drove off. I didn't stop. I noticed how the guards turned away the people who had hurried up and in panic I went to the dentist. After a few steps in EitelbergerStrasse-Hietzing Main Road, I looked round and saw smoke rising from the synagogue. When I came back half-an-hour later I saw the temple had been burnt out. Stella [niece][7] and Fritz [adopted brother][8] were standing in front of my house and told me I should not go into my flat, bands of Nazis were breaking in everywhere, smashing and stealing, arresting the men. How lucky it was that I was not at home, they had already come to the front door twice. I spent the day until night time with Richard [best friend][9]; then left, walking along the BösendorferStrasse, I got home towards 10:00 o'clock. The next day the news filtered through: several synagogues had been destroyed, as well as the mortuaries of cemeteries; thousands of men had been assaulted, arrested, dragged off to the Dachau and Buchenwald camps. Unspeakable misery – the same had happened in the whole of Germany – perfectly organised. Hanna [sister][10] and Stella [her daughter] left the next day for Ostrau[11] – they had also suffered from a hooligan gang at their place. Today I realise that they went, unfortunately, from the frying pan into the fire – they have experienced a terrible year – where are they today? Gone with the Wind. The fear and terror is that these bands of criminals will repeat these actions in some form on this day of remembrance; particularly after the assassination attempt.[12] Investigations into the assassination attempt are so far unsuccessful. The Germans say that England, and of course the Jews, are behind it.

16 November 1939

Hansl received his exit permit today. We are leaving, intend to leave (what can you know nowadays) on the 26 November. I want to accompany Hansl to the ship on 2 December. Hopefully I can move to Petts Wood so I don't feel quite so alone. I am sleeping very badly, disturbing thoughts are going around in my brain – it is only nerves.

19 November 1939

Well then, 2pm tribunal judge Arthur G.A., elderly gentleman. I was first on, handed in references from Jeanne Savage [English friend of his daughter] and David Kay [landlord]. He asked about my siblings, wife, children, job, the translation of the details of my pension given to the DDSH, whether I wanted to return to Germany, who would win the war. Answer Questions!…I am no prophet, hope and wish that the Allies will win. It lasted about 10 minutes. Then it was Hansl's turn. About 5 minutes later, called in again and with the words, 'he hoped we would be happy in England' we were dismissed as 'friendly aliens'.

20 November 1939

Sad letter from Ida written on the 13 November. The Yugoslavian visa has not arrived, probably they will leave for Palestine, if only they had already departed. Ida is most unhappy that we cannot be together. Will we ever meet again? No news from Hanna and Stella. Packed today and yesterday, day after tomorrow 10 a.m. departure for London. So ends the adventure of Manchester, I have managed seven months of the Manchester adventure, getting worse and worse! Since Saturday eight ships over 50,000 tonnes have been sunk, four English ones, four neutral. In Czechoslovakia more executions have occurred – poor mankind – what for, why? Life is senseless chaos and yet, read 'Faust' again, "I am gripped by the misery of the whole of mankind".

27 November 1939

So, yesterday we went first to Ida Kerner[13] [the Petts Wood clan are all relatives of his wife and Martin Bunzl], who lives in a small house very comfortably together with Lili Bunzl[14], daughter Liesl Pelc[15] plus granddaughter. Martin Bunzl[16] was waiting; we went to Mrs Durgan's [landlord] house together, 14 Crossway, my future home. Agreed the rent: thirty five shillings a week all-in – even laundry – four meals, breakfast, lunch, afternoon tea and dinner. The room is tiny: bed, cupboard, chair, but I may use the whole house, and work, write and read in the sitting room. I think it will be fine, the people make a good, nice, kind impression.

10 December 1939

Yesterday morning, at 8.20, Hansl left from Waterloo station to Southampton, to sail from there by the steamer *Veendam* to New York.[17] A difficult parting – at our home I had a good cry.

11 December 1939

This afternoon went to the police station at St Mary Cray to be registered, then home. Luggage has arrived, unpacked, put away, I'm now established.

30 December 1939

This afternoon at Schönbergs in Chislehurst – beef and a walnut cake that was cooked specially for me. Afterwards there was a chamber music quintet. First violin Dr Hain, second violin Friedl Schönberg[18], first viola Dr Pollak, second viola Koppel, cello Gustav Schönberg[19] – Beethoven, Mozart in G minor and a Haydn quartet in G. The Schönbergs live in a beautiful big country house, completely furnished with their Vienna belongings – for them nothing has changed. They have only relocated to a free country – to be appreciated, he was after all imprisoned for a few months. I don't know what job he does – he travels daily into town to Bunzl and Biach. All the musicians are Viennese, I wish Hitler could see how poor and rich Jews overcome their fate.

31 December 1939

New Year's Eve. From 10:30- 2:30 I went on a long walk with Mr Durgan and a friend whom we fetched from Orpington. From Green St Green to Farnborough – delightfully situated village. The district is hilly, woods, fields, meadows. Towards lunch time sunny, cattle feeding. In Farnborough, I visited a small old church dating from 1358 but damaged by storms on many occasions. Very nice old cemetery. I was back home in the afternoon. So ends the year peacefully. I'm content. If I think of last New Year, shortly after influenza, Lisl [daughter, now in Egypt] dreadfully ill, the terrible life after the 9 November 'what is all this sorrow and longing?'

1 January 1940

New Year's Eve: I was alone with Ida – an end-of-year celebration such as I have never experienced. Ida Kerner is certainly one of the cleverest, most cultured and kind women that I know. The content of our conversation: memories of our lives, reminiscences of the past year, persecutions, hopes for the future. At 10:30pm (German time 11:30) listened to the radio, caught 9th Beethoven symphony, 4th movement, final chorus (from Munich or Leipzig); listened in silence and was moved. Then the sound of bells which was immediately followed by Hitler. He read out a passage from Clausewitz[20] – fired up, rather than be defeated, honour is the same as might. After he'd spoken, they played the National Anthem and the Horst Wessel Lied. The text and music of the 9th which is about the brotherhood of man is incompatible with hate, the principles of Nazism. Clinked glasses of vermouth alone with Ida and spontaneously kissed. Went home at 1:00 and exchanged New Year greetings with the Durgans. Mother Durgan also hugged me and kissed me. And so two old mothers gave me kisses at the beginning of the year 1940. Is it an omen that I am on the threshold of old age. I read the following comment from the pianist Rosenthal: 'A man is young if he is rendered happy or unhappy by a woman, he is middle-aged if he only loves happily, and he is old if he loves neither happily nor unhappily'. Exactly my situation. Ida and I have helped our children to live, tears in our eyes.

21 February 1940

9:45pm. Today I am 67. I can view the past year positively compared with my previous birthday. God has given me health, I've escaped the hell of Vienna, I live, thanks to Hansl's initiative, carefree and peaceful, children are in good health…My only wish is to be united with my children, then to die peacefully.

10 April 1940

Yesterday afternoon with Ida Kerner and Else Wottitz[21] they wanted to talk politics and I refused. I advised them to avoid this topic and not burden themselves with worry about how it is going to end and to let events fatalistically happen. My opinion, which I only confess in these notes: Hitler is advancing unwavering and straight towards his goal to make Germany a world power. There is no doubt he is endowed with extraordinary abilities, like a fanatic who is dominated night and day with this thought, there is only the question whether this manner of thinking will prove well founded. Dogs are the death of hares. Up to now he has acted so cunningly, surprisingly adept, has been possessed of such energy that everything has been a success, just as he planned and anticipated. If the allies don't succeed soon in driving the Germans out of the Western harbours of Norway, the Germans will have the bridge to attack England. I can only, out of a purely personal standpoint as a Jew, pray that God will not let it come to this or that I will not live to experience it.

03 May 1940

Mediterranean on high alert – Allied cargo ships have been suspended; French /English fleet on the way to Alexandria. Now I am worried about Hans [Oppenheimer son-in law],[22] Lisl and Hannele [granddaughter] and Ida Kerner is worried about Bettina's [Ida's daughter also in Alexandria] family. It must be only a matter of time before Mussolini gets going. I often think to myself if I was not a Jew and if Hitler had not made his racial persecution a central plank of his programme, would I have followed him with great enthusiasm? The thought of a future German world power has always attracted me. How depressed I was, when we Austrians were forbidden after the end of the 1918 war, to join in union with Germany. If I recollect the conversations with my friend Edi Wibbe, how I, the Jew, supported and he, the German Aryan, opposed the Germans. How thoroughly I was mistaken about their characteristics!

12 May 1940

What is taking place in Holland and Belgium must be horrendous. The Germans are sending wave upon wave of airplanes over them, an uninterrupted hailstorm of bombs, they are landing soldiers everywhere, by parachute, that get a foothold and are then reinforced – with total disregard for any losses.

15 May 1940

It is impossible, as I've always reiterated, only to be an 'observer' of these events. I force myself to appear and remain calm – but everything is seething in me. Holland has surrendered; put down its arms – the Germans are utilising untold manpower in order to break through the Maginot line – what then? Let fate take its course. The day before yesterday I said to Martin Bunzl, 'are we going to have to wander on somewhere else again?' If Hitler (Germany) wins he will solve the 'Jewish question' according to his ideas – well-what then?

18 May 1940

The German war machine is working to perfection. They have broken through the Maginot line across 100 kilometres, have occupied Brussels; the attack with heavy tanks and low flying bombers seems to be unstoppable.

24 May 1940

Card from Albert [nephew][23], was imprisoned for 14 days and has been sent back to Germany – hopes to be able to travel to the USA in August/September if a journey is possible. According to statements from Churchill in Parliament the situation is serious – the sky is mercilessly blue, the sun is smiling, the birds are singing, everything is in flower – and people are killing each other. Several people arrested yesterday, Ramsay – obviously a traitor – leader of the fascists, Mosley and the whole leadership.[24] (I read to the end of '*Good God.*'[25] I must read it a second time more thoroughly. I found passages strangely reflecting my own thoughts: the thought of God cannot be personified, he is not bad or good, disinterested in our goings on in life; Christian belief is only 2,000 years old, ludicrously short time in comparison with the age of man, still in its children's shoes; convinced of constant development, set backs are only episodes, nothing is destroyed and out of ruins new worlds emerge.)

14 June 1940

It has happened more quickly than I expected, Paris has not been defended, has been handed over to the Germans today. The thought, that Hitler has achieved everything with systematic precision as he set out to do, is uncanny. Shall I really experience him raising Germany to the leading world power, realising on this planet his 'Weltanschaung' (a caricature of a view which denies all ethical advances of the last 2,000 years), or is the whole thing only an 'earthquake' which will give the communist viewpoint final victory?

25 June 1940

Yesterday, at 7:35am, the Italian conditions were accepted by the French and at 12:35 hostilities ceased. The Italian conditions have still not been made public. Today at 1:00am the first air raid alarm ended at 4:00am. I had been reading in bed and had just switched off the light when I heard the distant howling of sirens, which increased in volume. Suddenly the sirens sounded locally. Sat with the Durgans in my dressing gown in the dining room till about 2:30, read, then went back to bed and fell asleep and slept through the all-clear signal. I can't say that I was upset – first test – it will probably be repeated now many times.

27 June 1940

Sensation, since yesterday morning I have been interned.[26] At 8:30, I was in the bath, and a detective appeared, giving me an hour. I informed Ida Kerner, who was to ring Dr Jesner for him to examine me and declare me unfit – all in vain. Taken by car to St Mary Cray where I met up with Karl Weiss [another Bunzl relative and his closest companion at Huyton],[27] then to Bromley to the police station where there were eighteen arrested people, including Gustav Schönberg and Dr Bach [medical doctor].[28] From there to the Chelsea barracks, to a school, a collection point for some 100 of us. From there by bus to Kempton Park, a racecourse, great confusion – about 1800, I'm group number 28/2 number 1428 so I have finally, at the age of 67, become a mere number.[29] All valuables, documents and knives were taken off us. Books and writing materials, after inspection by an officer, were returned thank goodness. This is only a transit camp. We are to move on in about two days' time. Given a mattress and two blankets, we slept close to one another on the ground. Morning ablutions were quite difficult, a crush, not much fun but could be worse. I took my leave of the Durgans with kisses. Todge [the dog] was strange and would not go away from me – touching. In Chelsea, we received a good meat broth. In the afternoon we were given tea, bread and margarine and a small piece of cheese. Breakfast did not quite come off, a slice of bread and marmalade but no tea. 10:00am call up. I sent a postcard with pre-printed text to Martin Bunzl. No newspaper, no other connection to the outside world. I am curious how long this is going to last. The whole affair smells of a panic reaction. I gather it will be the turn of women soon.[30] One good thing- you know nothing about the outside world – yet quite interesting what I'm now going through – what next? So long as Lisl, husband and child and Gustidl are well.

28 June 1940

Yesterday many people were transported on. No new ones delivered – quiet day. In our quarters, I moved my place from the middle to the wall. It seems like a luxury because I now have a wooden ledge all the way round the wall on which I can store things: books, umbrella, gas mask and hat. Roll call was a somewhat stricter affair – lights out at 10:15 – we were advised to be careful if we went out at night because of the guards – to stand still if you hear your name, identify yourself as a 'friend' otherwise you'd get shot. Slept better. A young lad, who I take to be 16 years old, speaks in his sleep – partly in English, partly in German – asking for help and then sings again. This morning we had a big clean up, particularly the washrooms and WCs, high time. Toilet paper has appeared, great! Interesting to observe people at feeding times, like a menagerie. My neighbouring sleeping companions are a Dr K. former lawyer of the British Embassy in Vienna; Hellmann, employed by Shell in London; Dr Mayer,[31] likewise director in Vienna of a petroleum company which I dealt with; and, of course, Karl Weiss who has his bedding next to mine. Today bus after bus load arrived with 'goods', I've not seen anyone I knew. The most wonderful thing is the sense of relief – not to know about anything, a weight off your shoulders – number 1428 – formerly without much interest and now completely in the wilderness. I often have a tormenting thirst – bad, warm drinking water. Hopefully we'll soon be off and it will be better in the camp.

30 June 1940

Yesterday morning at 10:30, 645 of us were transported by a special train from Kempton to here, an alien internment camp in Liverpool.[32] The last noteworthy happenings in Kempton: the day before yesterday 'newcomers' arrived all day; on Friday evening and Saturday morning there were services in a specially designated hall. I became aware, as I was having my evening tea in the open air, of the Lekha Dodi[33] being sung. They are for the most part Eastern Jews but also many Germans. I did not participate but observed them from outside; fanatic faith, grim determination not to be eradicated even by 100 Hitlers. The journey here: arrived at 5:00pm in the afternoon, in the first class carriage, under military guard. Lunch time we had bread and a small piece of cheese, no water. At departure and arrival the older people were separated and transported by car to the camp which was half an hour on foot from the station, but I, who was one of the oldest, was not taken by car, apparently I looked too young, same fate in the camp here. Different atmosphere here, warmer more peaceful reception, only the top brass are militaristic. Most of the rest are interned Jews, very helpful and friendly, but it's a lousy set up. My group is in a large tent about twenty-five by ten metres. We were handed one rubber sheet for the floor, straw and straw sacks, a pillow case and four woollen covers. We had to fill the pillows and sacks ourselves, distribution lasted until 11:00 at night, didn't really work, the job was a bit much for me, I had heart palpitations, lay down for half an hour. Then went to wash – hot and cold water – in one of the houses/work barracks which was not completed, houses are finished but not furnished. Slept badly. In the wash house, I forgot my jacket and I thought my wristwatch, but could not find them. At 5:00am after searching, found the jacket without the watch, then looked in my bed and found the watch on the straw sack. There are over 3,000 aliens here, we are told that those of us in tents will soon be taken to the Isle of Man. My new number is 54919. Absolutely uninformed about what is going on, disturbed through tales and rumours; Russia apparently demanding the Dardanelles from Turkey, Hungary and Bulgaria have delivered an ultimatum to Romania. When I'm alone I sink into worries about the children, wrote to them. When shall I get the first news?

1 July 1940

Everything is relative. We were moved yesterday afternoon to a wooden barracks with wooden floors. A military barracks for twenty people – but we are forty-four; we lie pressed together like herrings. However, everyone is content not to have to lie on the bare earth and to have a roof over our heads. Otherwise nothing happened of significance. It appears we shall remain here a bit longer. There was news announced during our meal – I could have done without it – that, in an air battle, the Italian Air Marshall Italo Balbo was shot down and the whole herd cheered with enthusiasm, stupid people.[34] General Mittelhauser in Syria has placed himself at the disposal of General Weygand's rule.[35] The English have vacated some small islands (Jersey Islands). My internment is bearable as it is beautiful weather. Another 800 are due to arrive today, where will they put them? The camp is already over full. I am lying beside Karl Weiss; Gustav Schönberg has 'illegally' parked himself in a house nearer to Dr Hellmann (who is a commercial lawyer), Dr Mayer (the petrol industry), and Dr Vardig (lawyer).

2 July 1940

Yesterday arrival of 800, among them Dr Bach, who has been quartered in our barracks. The camp is to be enlarged, a third camp with a capacity of 6,000. The commanding officers have made their lives easy. They leave it to the 'prisoners' to sort things out to their satisfaction – self-government; it works quite well except for people who go off and do their own thing.

Everything summons up Jewish enterprise and a lot of noisy chatter. They are funny my Jews – without some 'business' they can't stand it. Everywhere there are the beginnings of business ventures, mostly: medical stations, a hospital, post office, a camp bank, and a lot of good healthy humour. Caricaturist Harald Lester (cartoonist of a Viennese newspaper) has a weather idea which has been published by the 'advertising' bureaux. In the main street, Parbrook Road, on every corner there are shoe polishers: the best one is a Viennese who attracts clients with his good jokes; one shoe 1/2d, a pair 1d. There are several 'hairdressers' – first class hairdresser 'West End'; laundries, one called 'Edelweiss' with an excellent shop sign, a mountain landscape – a cartoon tourist bent over an abyss, looking at one of his friends flying through the air whereas another is already lying face-down below beside his pick axe. The sign for the laundry called 'Star View' is a starry sky with a comet tail, text reading: 'it is already night but Star View is still washing'. Main laundry is 'Stern and Naussau', in a little room. The canteen is always crowded and so you are pleased to get something. There is an exchange, optimal rates, where you can advertise: 'new razor blade sought in exchange for five cigarettes', 'a pair of socks for two ties', ten words for 1d. Great drawings entitled 'From the town's cultural life': 'This is my Freedom' in which a plucked raven sits crying on a twig, saying: 'He who digs a hollow groove for another has gold in his mouth and in the morning falls into the hole himself'. There is Camp Porridge University; a gym/keep fit programme by practical training; a tailor; a shoemaker; and, particularly popular, is 'Chance' who offers to do the washing up, do your clothes or shoes or carry water. The 'hotel' is in one of the workers' houses: no opportunity to snack but for a very high payment gourmet food is advertised, breakfast 4s 11½d Dinner 6s 9¼d. Also alcoholic beer, schnapps and wine – of course it is all a joke. There is a billing of a show – the 'Virgin Girls'. Turnover, with the exception of the restaurant, is in pennies. We still cannot write letters, this will last a few days more, we will be allowed twenty-eight lines. This afternoon met Robert Koch, he spent about a year with a farmer, his parents and brother Walter are still in Vienna. Robert has been in the camp for seven weeks. Last night in his barracks there was the first suicide, a man by the name of Schiff, 59, from Breslau, who was depressed. He had a wife and two married daughters, a son-in-law who is a professor at Oxford and another in the Army.

3 July 1940

Yesterday some 600 single internees, between the ages of twenty and forty, were transported to the Isle of Man, having been here for different lengths of time, among them Viktor Bunzl[36] and Robert Koch. Yesterday evening Dr Rosenberg came to see me through Dr Bach. I was, as ever in such matters, really stupid. A general move to get on the ferry began immediately in the house. Dr Hellmann advised me to wait. Missed the ferry, didn't find anything, went for a test, inquired about a move due to my heart condition, couldn't read the report, was sent around from one person to another. Finally found an office, closed, no one working there today. I was comforted by the thought I could go tomorrow. Everyone else I know has managed things through being alert and clever. I'm a 'nincompoop'. Writing letters is still not allowed, have no money – keep smiling.

5 July 1940

There has been another suicide overnight – yesterday a new transport arrived from Kempton Camp. In the afternoon we waited again in vain for 2 hours on the parade ground for money distribution. Broke off at 6:30pm, apparently because a young chap had made some comment (quite right too). There is a rumour that a large transport of 1,000 is due to leave within a day, according to Professor Weissenberg,[37] Nobel prize winner. There was an excitable meeting under the direction of the 'street fathers' (house fathers, street fathers and camp father).[38] Talk of a resistance organisation, complaints, demands that at deportation women can come too and for internees not be transported on their own. Nonetheless people cannot always moan and nag. Amusing posters are being produced by Walter W. beautifully dumb. In the evening, in the first tent, there was a cabaret evening and a concert, a bit of rubbish apart from the pianist L. (from Vienna) who played really well. The compère was a certain Miller from Vienna, he is said to have been a manufacturer of tins, fat chap, quite funny. It wouldn't be at all bad if I was to be sent free of charge to Canada. My long-felt wanderlust to see the world would be satisfied in my old age. I should be grateful to Adolf, that I am able to experience that, 'nebbish'. Otherwise I would have lived on in Vienna with worries until my death.

6 July 1940

Yesterday at last I got some money 10s 6d – paid my debts, bought bread, sardines and tobacco, filled in forms and handed them in with exact dates. There is a question on the form about whether you want to go overseas or remain in England and the reasons. To the last question I answered that I wanted to remain, reason age and illness. I can hardly write. I sit on the ground with my blanket with a case as support. Again there was a suicide, a 68-year-old man. There are rumours about a sea battle involving the English and French fleet in Oran, most of the French ships were sunk, one battleship, the Strasbourg, and two destroyers got away.[39] In Alexandria, French ships were confiscated. The English are said to have more than 60% of the French fleet. Diplomatic efforts between England and France have broken down, it's all shit. This morning I did not feel well, heart palpitations, settled, better now. Franz Goldberger and Georg Schapinger[40] have come. Rudy Bunzl[41] has been released and went to London, he is going with his parents to Brazil.

7 July 1940

There are rumours that men over sixty are to be set free, Jewish women are said to have demonstrated in London in front of Bloomsbury House.[42] The leading papers (*Times*, *Daily Telegraph* and *Manchester Guardian*) have written articles attacking the shameful handling of the refugees. General Motors (Detroit) have threatened to stop war deliveries to England if there is no change in policy. Henderson[43] is said to have agreed in Parliament to take action to find a solution. The administration of the camp is to be transferred from the War Ministry to the Home Office. If you go out onto the streets you hear nothing but the imagined speculation of desperate minds – my God, how sorry I feel for mankind – how they struggle like flies in a web.[44] I try in our room to generate a sense of the ludicrous which finds resonance with Karl Weiss and Dr Mayer. The latter put up a notice yesterday on the reception board of Camp 2, 'Salzamt Eröffnet – Tent 999', a joke which only the Viennese would understand.[45] The German Jews are puzzled about what kind of new office this is. Spoke to Franzl G. Wrote to Hansl, I wonder if the letter will arrive?

8 July 1940

Cleaned up the room, one drowns in dirt. Have not bathed since the 25th, I cannot sit in a bath in cold water. I have ordered two buckets of hot water for 6d for tomorrow. Have no money, borrowed half a crown from Ing. Fischer[46] (who is the father-in-law of Gustl Bunzl).[47] I asked permission to withdraw £1 from my post office savings book – will only get it next week on Thursday. Yesterday afternoon in the fresh air, Mittler[48] started reading Faust in front of a small circle of intellectuals, very good. In the evening a concert, Professor Hochstein(?) (a piano teacher in Vienna) technically good but not a musical pianist. A singer, Elkan, pleasant but weak voice, without depth or range: Ständchen by Schubert, Cradle Song by Brahms, the Osiris Aria from the Magic Flute, low notes totally out of tune but I was thankful to be somewhat distracted. In the evening a conversation between Dr Mayer and Karl Weiss – Dr Mayer, the giant (1.90 metres), obviously an extraordinary disadvantage, fell in love as a student with a rich girl who Karl also knew well, her father was against the marriage – in the ditch, a fight between the two of them, till both were bloody, taken off by the police. He then married another girl – love marriage, married for two years – returned from a business trip to Rome to find the flat empty, wife left him with his cousin Dr Lederer, a twenty-year-older man. Mayer is divorced and now again married with a younger wife aged twenty-six. Dr Mayer is a problematic individual, very cultured, a talent for languages, witty, good natured, but makes a fool of himself and the world. The French fleet in Alexandria has surrendered. Gibraltar has been bombed by the German, Italian and French (surely a joke) planes.[49]

9 July 1940

Had the first register, my registration cards were missing, yesterday applied for new ones. Again told to go to bed by the doctor, trying his best- in the afternoon a young doctor, Dr S., at the instigation of Dr Mayer saw me – none of it will be of any use. Everyone under 50 is said to be going abroad, those who applied by 08/09/38 for emigration are included, even if they are over 50. Women and children are to be sent on, money transfer is possible. Lists are due to be completed today. In the afternoon I attended an English lesson in tent number one by Prof. Hirschhorn, from the Ottalinger Gymnasium School – very good. Then bridge with Gustav Schönberg, Schapinger and Karl Weiss. In the evening, a piano concert in Parbrook Road, excellent: Schubert, Beethoven Sonatas, Stravinsky – the latter, modern and atonal, ruined the impact of the sonatas. The tent was bursting full, about 1000 enthusiastic listeners, parents, members of the singing academy – the pianist was very musical, mother was born at Kurzwald,[50] an old Jewish Viennese family, uncle is a well-known conductor. Karl Weiss is a good chap, always cheerful although he obviously suffers a lot of pain. I believe he has spinal atrophy. I asked if I could draw cash from Gustav's postal savings book. The sports department is managed by the Viennese heavyweight champion, from Oberland. He is about thirty years old, a giant of a man, with arms like my thighs and legs like columns. There are daily football games, the day before yesterday,

Austria v. Germany, Austria won by 12:3. During the game the spectators called out: 'Wake up Germany!'

10 July 1940

No ink to be had anywhere. The camp yesterday was like a swarm of bees before their flight. The list of those 1,200 prisoners designated to travel overseas had to be completed and, as there were not enough volunteers, the missing numbers were selected ex officio. Among them were fifty-five year olds, married people who have lived here for years and built up a life for themselves. There seems to have been a lot of patronage in play, a black market has developed, you pay up to £20 for an exit visa. I had ordered 6d of hot water for a bath in the afternoon but it was not delivered. Washed myself in cold water and soap - leg looks bad.[51] In the evening a request concert by Londoners – Schubert, Chopin, Puccini. Today a departing transport, at the last minute Dr Mayer decided to go with them, interesting – sad to watch the internal battle in the divided mind of this 190cm tall man- a mixture of energy and childishness. From the house M. Finkle and a certain Fisson left, and amongst my acquaintances Dr K[52] (59 years old). In the faces of the departing travellers one could read all human emotions. Among the young mostly there was thoughtless unconcern, among the older ones resignation and despair. In addition it was raining. Leave taking from Mayer and Dr Philipp was hard – to see the big man crying – I must keep smiling. The millions of Dutch, Belgian and French citizens had a far worse time. Mayer and Philipp gave me the addresses of their relatives and a post restante address in order to receive their letters and parcels, to take out any food and forward their post. Yesterday, I took out £1 of Gustav's money.

11 July 1940

Yesterday, I forgot to mention that an older man in one of the barracks attempted suicide through poisoning, saw him being taken out unconscious. Cold rainy weather, you sink in the mud. The worse scandal is there is no WC paper, the feeling that I'm running about so dirty and filthy is not pleasant – hope I don't become ill. This morning I remained lying down and had unpleasant heart palpitations and breathing difficulties – keep smiling. Gustav Schönberg has received a food parcel, he gave me and Karl some of it, tongue, fruit and condensed milk – so folk live – the animal in us is satisfied. In Parliament the head of the refugee committee,

Eleanor Osborne[53], made a strong complaint against the treatment of the internees – she demands that those responsible justify themselves. M.P. [Osbert] Peake rejected this on behalf of the Home Office and the War Ministry.He said that a Ministerial Committee under the direction of Chamberlain was looking at the treatment – M.O. Pirth[54] seems to be correct when he says that Chamberlain is a secret Fascist. The Fascist Party is forbidden in England, likewise in their newspapers.

In the Channel a big operation of 200 German planes attacked the convoys (of English soldiers still in France),[55] fourteen were shot down, others damaged, no Allied losses. Four Swedish torpedo boats, bought by the Italians, have been captured by the English. Done directly, and then compensation given to the Swedes. The Turkish Parliament has been summoned, discussion about the Dardanelles at Russia's request. Estonia, Latvia and Lithuania have been absorbed by Russia.

Ernst K. tells me that those over sixty-five are to be released in the next few days. Mittler is 'organising' an agreement by all the people with technical qualifications and then wants to hand in the collective application to the Ministry of Supply, and offer our services. He hopes they will say: 'We were waiting for your offer'. At 5pm it was announced that a ship for refugees would depart for Australia. The Australian Government has offered to take in 6,000 refugee families and there are 750 places left. Married couples may apply until 8:00pm tonight. When I went past the application office at 6:00pm there were already hundreds queuing in front of the office, the poor weak-minded are beside themselves.

12 July 1940

Camp organisation is becoming more and more ridiculous. Yesterday evening supper was meant to be at 5:30, half the tables and benches have been moved out into the barracks – only half the internees were able to sit, and added to that, the second sitting was marched in – it was absolute chaos. Finally at 8:30 we got our tea consisting of bread, margarine and marmalade. In contrast at home we had a regal alternative through Schönberg: we had tinned tongue, tinned fruit which we shared together with Austerlitz – the joys of a full stomach generate a good mood. Chatted until 11:00pm. This morning the same muddle, breakfast instead of being at 7:30 only took place at 9:30 – no porridge, rotten weather, it's raining cats and dogs – but again a feeling of pleasure – we, Karl and I, have obtained a roll of toilet paper, price 7d, twice the normal price. There is nothing to be had in the canteen apart from bread. There is an article in the *Daily Herald* by Noel Baker about the internees.[56] It will take a while but there are to be new 'test' committees. I was in two minds at lunch time whether to go and eat – it was pouring so much – all of us lounge about on our straw sacks having taken our shoes off. Karl Weiss is a good man, keeps on joking inexhaustibly – well, and I? – I try to keep going, sometimes it requires a great effort, what is the point of this whole nonsense?

13 July 1940

Yesterday evening a transport of 100 men, aged between 60 and 70, from various camps arrived. Our house father – also the union secretary of an association of commercial trade unionists, Dr Gottfurcht[57] – announced at the evening house meeting that the list of those wanting to go to Australia has been declared invalid. A new list with worse conditions will be drawn up by 11:00 today. Category 1: married men whose wives are interned on the Isle of Man; Category 2: married men whose wife and family live in London; Category 3: those whose wife and children live elsewhere. The transport will be in the same convoy but in different ships. Permission to live together in Australia has not been granted as there is no announcement from the Australian Government.

At the request of about forty Aryan German internees, the Swiss vice consul came to the camp, he was expected by the representative of the Germans and without being accompanied by the camp officers was allowed to wander freely and be shown round the camp. He is said to have said that he'd never seen such a miserable camp. Dr Weissenberg, the Nobel Prize winner, had an interview at the request of and in the presence of the camp Commandant. In answer to W's question, whether he represented the interest of the German refugees as well, the vice consul replied: 'Yes, all those with a valid German passport'. W. demanded specific assurances: whether German refugees were included, given the German Jewish laws – answer: 'I think only the German Citizens', whereupon W: 'Then, I have nothing more to say to you', quite right. The telegram addressed to Dr Gottfurcht confirmed that they had received his telegram adding that they will literally read it aloud in the Lower House, that the debate which we had been told about had taken place, and that a Parliamentary Commission will shortly be coming to the camp. W. collected reports of the individual specialised organisations and the camp activists (doctors, commercial people, kitchen staff, workers, personnel etc.). Stephan Mittler is to hand in a report in the name of the technicians. Dr G. has summarised the wishes of our house, it will be handed over. This morning Gottfurcht told me that he believed I would soon be released. An influential English lady, who was here on a visit, said the internment of a C category would not be applicable and new tribunals would take up their role in the camp. On the parade ground nothing special. I think that the Germans are preparing the attack against England. Unfortunately there is still no news.

14 July 1940

Nothing special. Yesterday I sent birthday greetings to Hansl for the children, Lisl will be 31 and Hansl 29. I would never have believed it possible, that I, surrounded by barbed wire, would experience this birthday of the children as a prisoner. My heart pains are becoming more frequent. From tomorrow on we are to receive newspapers, the house has ordered them collectively, *Manchester Guardian*, *Daily Telegraph*, *Sunday Times* and *Picture Post*. Karl W. has received a parcel, clothing, food. I wonder whether or when the food requested from Martin will arrive? Karl and I, together with our room-mate Austerlitz, who is a perfect Englishman, are reading one hour daily and translating the book *Good God*[58] which Austerlitz has already read with great interest.

15 July 1940

Big Day. Did my washing, for 6d had two pails of hot water delivered by a kitchen lad. During lunch in the tent there was an air raid alarm, lasted about forty minutes, distant sound of gunfire. At 3:45 we had an inspection by Captain Smith, could also be called a visit. We were alerted in the afternoon, our house father, that a sudden visit was about to happen, we were to make our stolen bench disappear. Karl and I quickly got it to the ground; I over-exerted myself, painful heart, lay down until lunch time, felt better. By the way, Gustav Schönberg had a giddy spell as we left the tent this morning. The barter business is booming, money-free exchange, six cigarettes for one handkerchief, my golf shoes against some trousers etc. Gustav Schönberg received two letters from home; his letter written on the same day as mine is still not in the hands of his wife. Weather, thank God, is warm.

16 July 1940

After an 8-day interval spoke to Franzl G. He seems not to be in the best of health – very depressed. Received letter from Otto Hirschhorn[59] dated 23/06 from London (sent via the internment camp address) was stamped on 09/07. Collapse of one business undertaking, the newspaper smuggler, because newspapers are now allowed in. People complained very bitterly as for every secret newspaper reading you had to pay up to 3d. Ing Fischer, the father-in-law of Gustl Bunzl, had a telegram from Hugo Bunzl[60]- they are all free – trying hard to get him out.

At lunch yesterday an announcement was read: an Aryan (Nazi) German group has been formed under the leadership of a certain Gunther – apparently a Sudeten German from the kitchen staff. A man of about 50, spoke animatedly against it, called all its members 'filth', was interrupted by a Nazi group on the next table to mine. The man however did not give up, he went over to the table and said to one of them 'we know you all and you, in particular, look out': the man did not bat an eyelid. Of course the English are once again too fair. I have no doubt that the fellows are spying and smuggling out information. And the stupid, cowardly Jews – this will be their best opportunity to beat up a few Nazis. A weak revenge for the horrors they have caused. In the evening, had a conversation with our house father Hans Gottfurcht who has some quite interesting experiences of his own regarding the actions against him by the Gestapo – the interrogations.[61] Received a telegram that he will soon, through the interventions of the Labour Party, be released. In the Shepton Road, there lives a young painter, Dachinger,[62] by name and appearance a pure Aryan type who has painted the walls of his five- person-occupied room with very good naked women, a family picture! His room-mates have made a table out of stolen wood, an armchair for the house father, three chairs and a self-made saw. They are a lot of jolly young lads, four from Vienna, one German- I think if I were young I would manage to do some useful and good things. But now I am an old invalid observer. Today it is three weeks since my arrest, time races by. At our dining table, Dr Erlangen,[63] apparently one of the leading lawyers in Munich, lawyer to the Wittelbachers and Hohenzollerns, about 60 years old, very cultured, and in contrast to Gustav Schönberg, an amusing raconteur. I should have received money yesterday from my deposited money, stopped[64]. Apparently because they have discovered that people are controlling large sums that are smuggled in.

17 July 1940

Wrote to the Durgans. Gustav has a letter from Martin who writes that he has intervened on my behalf concerning an affidavit for Hansl. From Harry H, a letter with copies of the correspondence with Weinberger concerning Stella's money.[65] Haifa has been bombed for the first time by the Italians –

three wounded – now Gustidl are in a danger zone. Martin B. appears not to have received my letter yet, can't understand it, as the letter from Karl W. has already reached him. Perhaps because it was written in German? Today peeled potatoes with 50 others. I now read the paper daily, skim through it, it repels me. From Sunday onwards, they are to introduce 'camp allowances' – I'm afraid of bribery by the camp soldiers.

18 July 1940

Yesterday afternoon the street leaders were invited, under the leadership of Dr Weissenberg, to tea with the new Commandant[66] – nothing concrete – his authority is internally focussed, it doesn't go beyond the barbed wire. He is said to be shocked at the state of our camp. He has great experience. He comes from the Isle of Man where there are 10,000 internees. He will do his utmost to bring some order. We are to prepare ourselves for a long stay. In the house discussion it was pointed out that the most pressing needs were: a table and chairs in every room; light; heating; cleaning materials (cloths and broom); bath – and only then cultural matters like cinema, reading room, canteen etc. Two letters from Hansl from 9/06 and 19/06 – not very satisfactory as he takes events very much to heart and is very depressed – worries about the family, Lisl, Gustidl etc. At his work an unpleasant incident, $40 and then $80 went missing, the thief has not been discovered – they even suspected Hansl at first – it seems to have been sorted, his pay has gone up by $3 a week. Yesterday I had an unexpected parcel from Grete Bunzl [Martin's wife] she had not had any news or requests from me – sweetmeats (Linzer torte, chocolates, cake) very kind. A culinary treat!

19 July 1940

Received letters from Hans Popper [67] and one from Laufer[68] with a copy of the letter from Hansl to Gustidl to whom he has given an affidavit. The letter is from 09/07 from New York – quicker than a letter from here to London. Two parcels from Petts Wood – washing, shoes, a string of thin sausages, a packet of food to Dr Philipp which I have used for myself as instructed. Ample provisions – all, of course, donated as presents – the people live. Dr Bach wanted to take me (and some volunteers) to the chief medical officer, Dr Williams, to discuss my release: it has not happened. It is said we are to receive beds, tables and chairs – I don't believe it. The Bishop of Chichester and the Chief Rabbi[69] as well as the Attorney General from the Home Office visited, they are said to have had a very frank discussion.[70] A new agency for sale and exchange has announced, written in pencil, a daily news story – quite important – I shall collect them.

20 July 1940

I'm sick and tired of these house father meetings. Gottfurcht, this trained facilitator, reports briefly, clearly, articulately then the crazy questions and discussion begin, particularly stupid among the suggestions are the 'demands' of the intellectuals, especially Mittler. He was an ARP (air raid precaution) warden, gives us a lecture with minimum understanding of current circumstances and what is needed, does not consider in any way that he is an internee. Gottfurcht reports that postal communication has been established with Switzerland. Mittler then asks Gottfurcht why England does not redirect the post via Spain or Portugal, whereupon I break up the debate by directing Mittler to headquarters. However, what is really important is that if a bomb attack should take place there is nothing in place – the wounded would have to die as even the most basic rescue measures are absent. The English chief medical officer has been replaced by an internee doctor. In the morning a young doctor arrived who prescribed a second straw sack to enable me to place my leg higher at night. These gentlemen Israelites will not allow themselves to feel defeated – language lessons in English, French, Spanish, Russian and Hebrew. Various lectures: the planned economy; physics – atom theory; historical short talks – all well attended, mostly by younger people in the spirit of knowledge being power. The intellectual appetite is not to be suppressed, even if Hitler began his address to the Reichstag yesterday by saying that Jews had caused the war. Two more parcels, an 'overall' suit, fantastic from L.[71] via Martin, goodies – bacon, pork crackling etc. from Gustl, simply great. Two packets for Dr Philipp, only clothes and rubber shoes, I can send them back. Today a Parliamentary Commission under the leadership of MP Rathbone was here.[72] Wrote to Mrs Joyce Constant, thanked her for Dr Mayer's cigarettes. Karl Weiss wrote at my instigation asking Martin B. to give me five to ten cigarettes as an advance on my funds. Once a week, every Tuesday one cigarette is to be paid off until the age of 70, on the 21 February 1943, 85 weeks – a joke which I hope will go down well.

21 July 1940

Sunday: to celebrate this day of rest Karl and Austerlitz did not get up. I brought home their breakfast bread – a pre-breakfast at home – pork crackling- are we in a bad way? After breakfast there was a meeting of the house fathers, Gottfurcht reported about yesterday's discussion with MP Rathbone, nothing concrete, words, words, words – we are not forgotten. You can make enquiries to a particular advisory office that has been newly established in London by the Home Office regarding release-I will do this. I will wait until after the speech by Anderson on Tuesday.[73] Forms have been sent around to provide statistics establishing the number of refugees, which I take to be a secondary measure ordered by the Camp Commandant – but the clever dicks sniff the danger of Hitler and they don't want to hand in their bits of paper. In the morning at 11:00, Dr Ing Glaser, whom I know by his publications in the VDJ,[74] visited. I offered food from my supplies and we had a cheerful breakfast with bacon, sausage and breads. Agency 17 has put out some notices: offers are on the rise but demand is low; margarine is very much in demand; weekly advice offered; women hairdresser sought; today's noon change was prolonged, something unfolds tonight. Overall they are excellent.[75] Everyone envies me. From Gustav, fine Dutch cigars, a Sunday treat. Our window looks out onto the canteen used by the soldiers. When the door is open you can see them sitting contentedly having a beer, and hear them singing – a disadvantage of our house!

22 July 1940

Yesterday evening there was a football match played near the barracks. Almost all the players were Viennese. Amongst the spectators were English officers and soldiers who had access to the camp or were part of the team – joyous. An English sentry with a gun – who was standing guard at the barracks behind the pitch, twice kicked back the ball, which had landed behind the goal posts, to the goalie – only in England could this happen. I sent on two parcels to Dr Philipp. Gustav Schönberg has moved to the special diet hostel.

This is the layout of our room. The bedroom and sitting room are separated by cases that have been stood on end. The 'lounge' is lined with newspaper on the floor. Entry to the bedroom is achieved by climbing over the cases and is only allowed in socks or stockings. The bench – a long plank laid on bricks – almost inevitably collapses through the movement of the upper body. The table is made from the planks of stolen crates nailed together, covered with a cardboard surface. Ante room only for 'lay-men', lounge for saints, only in socks. On the wall in the lounge we have posters: 'take no thought for the moment for the morrow shall

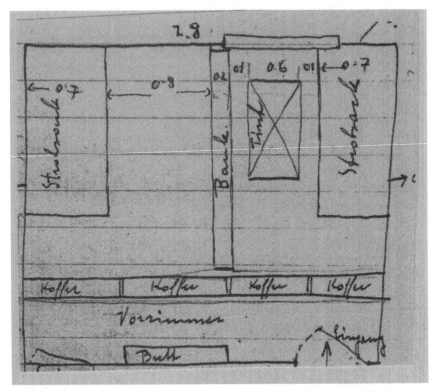

Sketch of the layout of the room, Wilhelm Hollitscher's diary, 1940, Wiener Library
Eingang= entrance, Brett= Plank, Vorzimmer= sitting room
Koffer= suitcases, Stronsack= straw sack, Bank= bench, Tisch= table

take thought of itself: sufficient unto the day is the evil thereof'. 2. 'The time is out of joint. O cursèd spite, That ever I was born to set it right!' (Hamlet). 'Wonder while you still have the light otherwise night will descend when no one can act.' Wall B: 'Imperious Caesar, dead and turned to clay, Might stop a hole to keep the wind away. Oh, that that earth, which kept the world in awe, Should patch a wall to expel the winter's flaw!' 2. 'For what shall it profit a man, if he shall gain the whole world and lose his own soul?'

Every evening before bedtime there are discussions. I'm amazed and entertained again and again about the intellectual preoccupation (Jewish) of these nebbisch[76] – who are so self-important. Gottfurcht is one of the most respected, he believes everything that he says and treats others as fraudsters.

23 July 1940

Yesterday evening there was a concert in Hut 1: two brothers, one a pianist and the other a violinist. They played Bach, Beethoven's spring sonata, Mendelsohn's violin concerto – good. I introduced Gottfurcht to Dr Ing Glaser, from Vienna who has been here since 12 May,[77] a pioneer in the building of the camp, a founder of the bank, now creator of the kitchen, looking for an organiser with cooking experience. Yesterday afternoon there was a row between the kitchen administrator Dr F. and the stores keeper Schmidt. Eight people with difficulty kept the two apart- those Jews! Karl did some 'washing', my pyjamas too. I had not thought how he does the washing; he does it by swishing his underpants through the cold water, then he holds them up against the light- if they are transparent – he is highly satisfied, chuckles happily and hangs them up without wringing.

A postal scandal! Yesterday 90 letters were distributed among 3,700 internees – it is said that more than 14,000 letters are lying around in Liverpool. Today a demonstration should have taken place in front of the Commandant. The Commandant left for London in order to find out the reason for the postal delay.[78] Letter from Richard Kann sent on 13/06. They are very well – were invited over the summer to Fish Island. Robert Kann, his nephew, has taken an exam as librarian. I have been moved from my tent to the eating hut where Schapinger is. It is much better, especially in poor weather. Tomorrow the engineering department is being constituted following a talk by Weissenberg about Herzl. We have an English conversation class in the morning. Someone spoke about Heine[79] and then a discussion about the concept of 'success' – not very good.

24 July 1940

Anderson spoke yesterday in Parliament denying reports, admitting that mistakes had been made. It looks as if people in my age bracket will be released in the foreseeable future. Wrote to Hansl. At 2:30 in the night there were renewed air raids, I lay awake for some minutes, did not hear the all-clear. Slept blissfully, meanwhile Schapinger sits fully dressed in the porch, the safest place in the house, simply incomprehensible. Karl W and Austerlitz, of course, stayed in bed and went on sleeping.

25 July 1940

Schapinger was taken yesterday afternoon to hospital, suffering from pneumonia – it is said that he will be transferred today or tomorrow to

Liverpool – poor chap. Yesterday afternoon, on the parade ground, there was a concert – some 150 listeners – followed by a talk by the Commandant, very sympathetic, a real English soldier – surely with the best intentions to help wherever and however he can. He always spoke about his 'fellow men'. The day before yesterday he was in Liverpool and collected 2000 letters. I received a letter from Ida Kerner, over the top praise – very kind. Also she has had a telegram from her daughter Bettina, saying that all is well – I conclude that Lisl, Hans and Hannele are also well. A card from Laufer, he got my address from Martin. I am to get a bed today and am apparently on the list of those to be released.

26 July 1940

Received letters from Richard Kann, Oppenheim[80] Harry Hollitscher, Martin and Grete Bunzl. The latter very kind. Richard is well, he has been invited, he is living in a nice country house, supplied with food, receives pocket money and there is a piano in the home. Oppenheim is ill, bedridden over the last fourteen days. He forwarded copies of his correspondence with Weinberger who has paid the first $5. Yesterday there was an air raid in Haifa, forty-six dead – Gustidl? Schapinger is in hospital in Liverpool, It is very serious. Yesterday I received a bed which I built up with the help of tiles which we broke out of a garden wall and stole. Furthermore we have bought a lamp – things are looking better and better. Yesterday afternoon, there was a meeting of the engineers – wholly uninteresting. Afterwards there was a lecture by Professor Weissenberg about the mechanical characteristic of materials, it was great. He is still a young man about forty, an interesting scholar. Again, a parcel from Martin: six tins of frankfurters with sauerkraut, a piece of Emmental cheese – touching. I have been told I am on the list of people to be discharged. Yesterday we got the stock market report – 'rain drops falling, balloons and rumours rising'. Since yesterday, I am having private English lessons together with Karl Weiss three times a week, taught by Dr Steindler at the cost of 6d.

27 July 1940

Received a letter this morning from the Durgans, and from Franz Tedesko[his wife's brother],[81] from 14/07, who has probably already had his operation. He was at Onkel Gustl[82] and Ida's, all well. His brother Karl[83] also has a cyst, the size of child's head on his left kidney and a large stone in his right kidney – poor chap that is why he has not been interned. This morning I had heart pains. I wanted to go to Doctor Williams, waited for two hours but wasn't seen. Hopeless organisation. A nice thing happened yesterday afternoon: about twenty older folk were sitting on benches peeling potatoes, with a young lad standing nearby with a harmonica helping the time to pass with Viennese music. In the evening I went for my first walk with Dr Rosenfeld – a serious conversation – he is very pessimistic with regard to the English – they are simply less capable than the Germans. He considered the treatment of the refugees an example of this in particular, and thought that they are fouling their own nest. A nice joke: 'Do you know why the English must win the war? Because the Gods themselves fight in vain against stupidity.' We spoke about historical materialistic interpretations, with which I disagree, based on the fact that there are no laws in history, and how ridiculous coincidences determine the fate of many generations etc. I spent the afternoon in Hut 3: bridge, with sausages – food break courtesy of Martin, and black coffee contributed by Gustav Schönberg – delicious.

28 July 1940

Nothing special. I'm going to risk expenditure and buy the postcards – caricatures by Baier. One is not allowed to send any smoking materials in parcels – only direct mail from the manufacturer,[84] you have to give in all your English money and are only allowed to use camp currency. Today I had my first warm bath – thorough cleaning, hair washing and pedicure – wonderful. The camp command is seriously discussing whether we should receive beer – the camp is gradually growing into a summer camp – some people who have been discharged have requested whether they can stay on. These people were living on benefits before and struggle with their existence – here they live free of worries, I can well understand it. I must sometime make a note of the dialogue between Mittler and Gottfurcht, it is wonderfully entertaining. Fritz Gross has asked for my autograph. He is collecting these from 'notable'(?) internees, wants to write about them. In Berlin and Rome, the representatives of Romania, Hungary and Slovakia are having talks with Hitler and Mussolini in order to fix the final borders – 'final'? Have the Russian agreed?

29 July 1940

Sunday lunch – sauce with beans – the colour already had an impact, I couldn't swallow them. Then we were given a pudding with custard – God have mercy on us! – a few bites – then everything in the bucket for pigs' swill. Back home to Emmental cheese with black bread, Linzer torte from Gustav Schönberg and his cigars – great. At 2:20 departed with others to the new football pitch about one kilometre from the camp, beautiful English countryside, lay in the grass for three hours, partly watching, partly dreaming looking at the sky. At 5:30 went back home for supper – tea with bread, cheese and margarine – a nice ending to the day. The youngsters organised a street concert in camp 3: there were two accordions, everyone in the circle around was singing and dancing, including all the footballers under the leadership of the heavy weight athlete Oberländer whose happy, good-natured, childish face, with its shining pale blue eyes, I could not stop looking at. Then suddenly a youngster of the Viennese type (of the Viennese Leopoldstadt Schilferl[85]) joined the circle and revealed himself to be a good whistler and singer – with an excellent sense of humour – if he is interrupted in the middle of his performance he whistles the well-known 'Ziag o'. I am – as you might say – immediately 'infected' and join in the singing and the whistling. Suddenly a young whistler standing beside me says: 'Listen, you should be in the circle as a solo singer'. I immediately stopped so as not to force Gustav to listen to me. I would only feel sorry for him and feel embarrassed – why? – to what end? In Bender's agency 'Stock market closed because of the threat of a bath day.' On Monday I will make big purchases: four sheets of writing paper, two trouser buttons, two pairs of darnable socks etc. – my own provisions are running out. I am very much hoping for a new delivery.

30 July 1940

In *Reynold's News*,[86] Wells[87] has written a red hot article beginning with the words of Zola 'J'accuse!'(Dreyfus affair) against internment. He accuses Fascist fellow-traveller governments of working for Hitler and Goebbels: at the end of these articles he writes that these fellows should be hung or shot.[88] The striking thing about it is that, nowadays, it makes no sense to publish such articles. Incidentally there are said to be camps where internees are worse off than in the German concentration camps – solitary confinement, exercise twice a day, hard labour and insufficient food. I have received a note written by the camp commander Captain Smith to Dr Williams, nonetheless I have not been summoned. Dr Zeelig took a note of my name and wants to interview me tomorrow morning, as the first patient. Yesterday, I had bad heart pains the whole day – I felt every cough. Today, I'm somewhat better although the night was bad. The Bendix Agency à la Christies has taken on a new role in Huyton. In one of the Huts, in Shepton Road, there is a notice that 'those that are not yet able to scrounge will receive free tuition from the house father'. A daily roll-call at 9:30 has been ordered.

The Pan American Conference has finished. It has been unanimously decided to prevent any change in the possessions of any European country, possibly to control the colonies and administer them jointly.[89] The USA is offering South American countries credit up to £125,000,000. The newspapers are boring – Germany is apparently preparing for a great offensive. This seems credible to me. It will be a terrible catastrophe if Hitler succeeds, then we Jews will have some frightful experiences before we are dead and buried. But there is time to think about this if and when events become more imminent. No news – no parcels.

31 July 1940

Yesterday afternoon we had a meal of sausages and in the evening a concert and recitations. Violin – good, a Polish Jew from Germany; cello was very good, name of Kuttenbach, obviously a professional. They played Bach and Beethoven's Variations on a Theme by Handel. There was a singer who rendered Schubert's songs with a weak, but not unpleasant, voice. I forgot to record in this diary that the day before yesterday I fell on getting up – knocked over the nearby bench and, of course, the worst thing of all, cut open my shin. Since yesterday we have changed 'the table' in our room. Today, finally, I was seen by the top doctor who examined my heart and leg, confirmed the diagnosis, put me on the sick list but my request for him to sign my application to be released was refused. I hope Franz Tedesko is on the way to recovery. I am dreadfully lazy – I could so easily be learning English – I live on mindlessly, I need to be uplifted!

1 August 1940

Wonderful cloudless, warm and sunny day – by God's grace – people breathe a sigh of relief, the faces are more hopeful, there is a glimmer of joy. The Shtetl[90] in front of our barracks is covered with sunbathing bodies. In front of me Gernus and Mittler are lying in their underpants. Karl W. is asleep. However that may be because he is the best sleeper that I know – he sleeps on his straw sack, fully dressed. I am only in my vest and underpants reading poetry. Today they have published the eight conditions for release. People under seventy are only going to be set free if they are invalids or suffering 'hardship'. After yesterday's consultation I do not belong to this category –

therefore there is little prospect of getting out. Yesterday evening there was a 'net-football' game, the star players were Weissburg, Freud and Müller etc. Some like Weissburg are quite good but Müller and Freud are jokes.

There was a march to the parade ground for exercise under heavy military guard, only 300 were admitted about 1,500 had to stay behind – I no longer take part – not necessary. The feeling of being a prisoner must be concealed. During the last walk, a certain R posted a letter openly into a public post box and was locked up for 8 days. He had wanted, by doing this, to demonstrate against the oppressive postal conditions. This is one of the greatest scandals: daily a maximum of 200 letters get distributed, whereas 6,000 letters are posted weekly which are surely answered. Thoughts of Gustidl, Hansl, Lisl, Hanna and Stella, and Hanspoldi [his brother Hans Jacob and wife Poldi][91] come to me and torment me more and more often. Hopefully Martin will send a telegram to Gustidl. The day after tomorrow Lisl turns 31, Hansl will be 29 on the 8 August, time flies.

2 August 1940

The punishment awarded to R. has been made public and walks and games outside the perimeter of the camp have been suspended. The postal scandal continues, letters from London take 14 days. Tomorrow five hundred youngsters from other camps are due to arrive – no hint of a mass release.

Molotov has given a speech, he has confirmed the alliance with Germany, good relationships with Italy and Japan have been established and Russia is unfriendly towards England. Goebbels has declared that the war has ended, apart from England, but it does not look good – I am waiting for a miracle to bring a change to the advantage of England. In Barracks number 3 there has been a big fight. The young Gabriel, when ordered to peel the potatoes, is said to have said that he would not do this for those 'damn Jews' – I could not believe this of the young man. The day before yesterday I posted an application to the Home Office Aliens' Department and a private stamped letter to Franz Tedesco. Both should have gone. I am having private English lessons, I could improve a lot more but I'm much too lazy, what's the point and why? I am tired. Today I got my writing paper, waiting to write, perhaps I will get something from Hansl tomorrow.

3 August 1940

Received a letter from Hansl 24/07 and at the same time a letter from Onkel Gustl posted on 18/07. In this way I celebrated Lisl's 31st birthday; I rejoice with news of them both, dear to me in their own ways. Hansl is trying to get an affidavit, has received a letter from Martin. His job is secure, he hopes to be promoted soon. Onkel Gustl is particularly dear to me. It is a good feeling to have such close friends. On Monday the Home Office is taking over control of the camp. I am curious to know whether the worst conditions, the post office and hygiene, will be improved- it occurs to me that normally nothing gets better. Gustav Schönberg has a letter from Martin who writes that I should seek release (have done so). The weather is lovely, therefore so is the world. Yesterday I had a beer banquet, a bottle which I drank with much enjoyment with a piece of black bread, the last slice, precious pleasure, 9d for a quarter of a litre. I replied to Hansl via Petts Wood, quicker and safer.

4 August 1940

Sent my letter off to Hansl via Martin. Yesterday afternoon, I attended a lecture, by Professor Hamburger who was a colleague of Einstein, about the problem of infinity in mathematics, very interesting.[92] In the evening I was watching the football on the small pitch, when a young man in his mid-30s addressed me, a Dr Nucki, the son Vitus Nucki and Marie, née Pisk, a cousin on my mother's side. His house father, a friend of Gottfurcht's, who has been watching me, had said I was a remarkably fit 67 year-old. I gave Dr Nucki my name, we exchanged memories, his parents are in Vienna. He, with wife, two children and two sisters, has already built a career as a dentist. Dr Nucki seems to be an intelligent chap, strange – in Vienna although I was on good terms with his parents, I'd never seen him. I have got to know him here, in an internment camp of all places! Today, the opening of the café Old Vienna in camp three, I went to have a look.[93] It's a charming room with colourful fresco pictures of this year's wine and a Danube steamer boat humorously painted. In the street there are about twenty tables with chairs, I imagine these will very soon be nicked – it is hard to see where these people have got them from. Weather continues beautiful. Two air raids at night. At the first one I got up, I was not yet asleep, in order to see something but thank God there was only a clear star-studded sky. At the second I hardly woke.

5 August 1940

Yesterday evening at 10:30 we had another feast: a tin of tomato herrings with a bottle of beer and then stewed plums – a Sunday finale. Today I was seen by a Dr Bilichheimer, at the recommendation of Dr Bonham. He will try to rectify the refusal of the English chief physician to let me go, which he finds incomprehensible. Dr R. informs me that Schapinger is dying, he has requested permission to inform his tenants by telegram, who knows what he is being spared – a lonely death? Hugo Dachinger is making a pastel picture of me. This afternoon was my first sitting, he says that I don't laugh and he finds my head interesting. In the afternoon coffee and cakes provided by Dr Piner, then a bridge game. Karl W. has a telegram. It looks as though, because of his permit as an exporter, he will be released. Otherwise unfortunately nothing from Petts Wood.

6 August 1940

Tettow has telegraphed today: 'I was told that friend Schapinger's state is dangerous in Whiston Hospital, Prescot' – perhaps Mr Tettow will drive there to visit. Yesterday we had a lecture about the Oxford Group, the movement of Pastor Schweizer, and his biographer Dr Kraus[94] – unsatisfactory since nothing was explained about the work of the organisation. It was a purely Christian movement founded by the American, Reverend Buchman, which challenged people to live according to the Sermon on the Mount: a categorical precept – absolute honesty and total submission. Kraus exonerated an end to prayer. We finished with the Jewish Blessing, '*Yevarechecha Adonai* – May the Lord bless and keep you'. I was interested in the matter because in 1936 when I was in Switzerland for a few days, I spent some time with the Head of the Department of Federal Affairs. On the way back to dinner with him, he told me about his unhappy marriage. Returning from a business trip, he found the house empty, his wife had absconded with his best friend. He was saved through the Oxford Group, living a pure Christian life and asking his rival for forgiveness. The Group was founded in 1922. My opinion: particularly in Europe this found fruitful ground because people in stressful times seek salvation in mysticism – religion, philosophy, astrology etc. Such mysticism is particularly effective with the unthinking masses. The historical proofs are the birth of Judaism or Christianity, Islam, Buddhism, the Reformation. If men were not such beasts, they would only have to follow the principles of the Jewish religion: the Ten Commandments; 'love your neighbour as yourself'; keep the Sabbath; seventh year sabbatical (release from your debt, a new furrow in the land). To revert to everyday life, the Jew-devourer, Streicher,[95] is said to have been tried and executed or ended his life by suicide. If only Adolf, with his colleagues Goering, Goebbels and Himmler could also have met this end, we Jews could have introduced a second national festival (Purim – Esther – Haman) as a festival of joy. Another dear letter from Ida Kerner, she had not yet received mine from 24/07.

7 August 1940

Yesterday at 6:15, I was summoned by Dr Jacobson who returned my application and told me I should write it out again and leave out my request to emigrate. It seems that Dr Bilichheimer has done his work. Finally he concluded that I should be in good spirits. My affairs look favourable – may it be so. From four to five in the afternoon, there was a lecture by Doring, who runs the most popular phonetic courses, about his experiences in Africa; amusing descriptions – he is an amazing fellow. In the evening in Hut 1 there was a Schubert evening. I sat outside on a bench and listened to the finale of the G sharp trio: piano, cello, violin. I received from Gottfurcht and Mittler the programme of all the lectures and courses running in the camp. It provides an interesting, as well as spiritually uplifting, example of the irrepressible Jewish intellectual force and energy (although a few Aryans can also be included). This enjoyment – spending the whole day and deep into the night going from one lecture to the next with an absolutely sincere, enthusiastic search for knowledge – unconditionally leads me to wish for an interesting conversation with Professor Liebert[96] – an exchange of views about the new world order, society after the war – involving philosophers in the whole world (48 universities). I have rejected such a proposal, being fully convinced about the purposelessness of philosophy, although Gottfurcht tells me that Plato said centuries ago that a proper world order can only be brought about by philosophy. Everyone forgets about the great mysticism in every person, the heart and brain and all that is connected to them. If people could keep to the Godly ethics of religion and live according to them, then we would not need all the speculations of philosophers. In any case, I follow the sayings of my father and I prefer a belief in God to the findings of the philosophers.

Had an airmail card from Gustidl from 23/06 and 01/07 – Ida has been ill and has had ten injections. I have had regular news from Lisl, but nothing from Hansl. A lovely letter from Ida Kerner. A card from Anny Winiewicz[97] from 07/06 she is in Montauban in France with all the P folk. Karl, her husband, has been interned in the vicinity of Bordeaux. From Hanspoldi there is good news and from Gustidl. Harry Hollitscher writes that he has had a negative reply regarding Gustav's money in Prague.

Addendum 7 August

In the morning between 10-11am, I was invited by Austerlitz to the Viennese café: coffee with cake and cigars, a cosy chat, having fun. Austerlitz paid. Yesterday evening in tent 2 there was a youth concert: folk songs sung in all manner of languages with guitar, accompanied by a harmonica and mandolin. In addition to German, there were songs in English, French, Italian, Hungarian, Swedish, Dutch, Bulgarian. There were no Russian songs. Austerlitz called it very enjoyable '*niedlich*'[98].

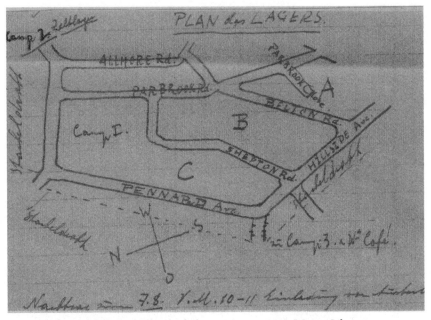

Plan of the camp. Wilhelm Hollitscher's diary, 7 August 1940. Wiener Library

08 August 1940

Hansl's birthday, God bless and keep him. I handed in a new application.

Last sitting for painter Dachinger – colourful, quite modern style. It is interesting for me because he sees me such as I am and not as I appear to the world. Of course only those that know me, like Richard Kann, know that. I look like a Prussian general – a strange resemblance to a photo that Hansl took of me after my first operation: more severe, more sombre, more suffering. My look – sharp features with high cheekbones. Dachinger wants to make a second sketch as does his friend, who, according to how he describes me, I also interest as an artist. Spoke to Dachinger's father, an observant Jew. We reminisced about the old Ferdermann in Bad Goisern am Hallstättersee. At the beginning of March 1919, Dachinger travelled to Goisern[99] to look for a summer residence and stayed at the Goisern inn. In the evening in the lounge, he could not believe his eyes when he saw beside the door the blue charity box of the Zionists with the Magen David.

As I sit here alone and reflect: Steffi B and Frau L, her boring sister, who have for weeks been recuperating in Goisern, appear in my mind. We greet one another happily and in answer to my questions I learn the following: The innkeeper is the illegitimate son of a Jewish subaltern who was banished to Goisern at the age of 14 and got by as a farm worker. As a young lad he had an affair with a 'prostitute' that produced a son. The mother died, Federmann brought up the son, a good result of a mixed race alliance. The son became well-to-do, married a rich farm girl who respects her father-in-law even more than her husband. Federmann works like any farmer – no stranger would believe that there is an 'interloper' in the house. He remains an observant Jew, prays daily, stops smoking on Friday evening (his daughter-in-law reminds him: 'Father it is *Schabbes*,[100] give up your pipe'). I often spoke with Federmann in the summer. He told me, like old Bachinger, that fishermen regularly came to Goisern for the Jewish festivals and stayed with him. He died in his late 80s in the 1920s, highly regarded, was buried in Catholic cemetery according to Jewish rites.

Two people from the house are searching for kindle. The others stand around and observe the preparations with lively interest, like small children. We exist within a total communist basic economy, since interest on money, wealth, possession do not exist. So the competitive motivation generating bad urges is missing. My colleagues' faces are lit up with happiness waiting for the successful event when the fraternal distribution of the individual portions of the kindle has taken place.

10 August 1940

Saw Dr Jacobson, my application went off yesterday. I received a letter from Martin which included a letter from Hansl. I replied requesting him to arrange for the Durgans to send a medical report to the Home Office. My meal companion, a Dr Hirsch from Mainz, came out with a nice aphorism: 'the present wave of persecutions demonstrates that the Jews refuse to be made into the proletariat'. At present we have some dogs and cats in the camp. How do people get to have them? The prettiest is 'Bimba', with who I am already on friendly terms. Today Dachinger and Rosen are beginning my portrait. Two letters from Hansl from the 20/06 and 08/07, which refer to a letter with cuttings that has not yet arrived. There has been a third theft in his office – money missing from the secure till. Hansl had again been suspected by the police inspector, but it seems to have been resolved, the brother of the female boss appears to have been the thief and has been dismissed. He used to have Hansl's position and was trying to get it back and carried out the thefts to cast suspicion on Hansl. I suppose I shall receive the letter with cuttings in the next few days. Wrote to Martin. There is no news in his letter about the health of Franz Tedesco.

11 August 1940

Yesterday afternoon in the tent I was approached by Glück, a trainee colleague of Hansl's in Salford, he was transferred five days ago from a camp near Manchester. He is an unpleasant fellow; he told me that he had sent me the third volume of the world history by Wells, which he had borrowed and not returned, an obvious lie. He even had the gall to write to me suggesting that I should send him some more books. Yesterday there was a nice concert in Hut 1, a trio in G by Schubert, three Brahms lieder sung by the chamber singer Ziegler, piano pieces played by Guttmann – Chopin, Brahms – and best of all a piano and trio. In the soldiers' canteen which is opposite my window, separated from us by a double-barred wire fence, I watched a Scottish soldier, accompanied by a mouth organ and a mandolin, sing wonderfully well and dance. It is great to observe the priceless English humour in the songs and dances. Dachinger made a sketch of me yesterday on newspaper working directly with colour. He certainly has talent – an immediate impression, not a true likeness, caught with concentrated observation. He intends to make another, Rosen was not present. This Saturday morning Karl got into a work rage. I was lying on my bed and was highly amused at how clumsy and disorganised he was. Suddenly the house father shouted 'roll caaall' which was drowned out by the dreadful singing of Kremers – whereupon Karl opens the door (which was not even necessary as you can hear whispers through the closed door) and roars out, my God, how he can yell with an extraordinary display of force and obvious satisfaction, a long drawn out 'rrrroll call'. I slept wondrously well all night – strange my heart quite still, yesterday it was painfully uncomfortable.

12 August 1940

Letter from Hansl of 15 July which has also overtaken the letter with clippings – its contents are quite good. Good news from Marianne [his wife][101]and Albert [nephew]. Marianne writes letters avoiding sensitive information which I receive within 11-12 days. The post, via Karl Tedesco no longer functions. Yesterday, on Sunday, we had a good lunch: boiled beef with cabbage, dried plums and figs for afters, followed by a wonderful black coffee in our house on my chest of drawers with Karl's coffee and cake and each of us smoked one of Martin's cigars. We ate lying on our beds-the purest idyll. In the afternoon, coffee time was in my Hut; followed by a bridge game. Lili the donor of the walnut cake and Else, donor of the nut pastries, were toasted with love (why not? We male mammals register love through our stomachs). In the evening read Ensor's History from 1780-1914.[102] This morning bathed and had a room wash down by a kitchen lad, a heavy task. He had to fill his bucket five times with fresh water. Apparently this is the first thorough clean of our room since the camp was founded six months ago. Beat out my and Austerlitz's blankets and straw mattress in the open air. If life were to become more luxurious, my optimism would be unbearable. Ing Fischer told me yesterday that I act on him like a ray of sunshine; when he sees me he is always lifted out of his depression and becomes cheerful and of some use.

Yesterday, Lord Lytton,[103] chairman of the advisory council on the welfare of refugees, paid a visit to the camp. He had a long discussion with the representatives of the camp in the presence of the Commandant, some officers and received a presentation regarding hygienic and medical conditions by Dr T Lord. Dr Lord was very well informed and well disposed towards the internees – no doubt there was no positive outcome but it is a good thing that representatives of the Government visit regularly and submit reports to the authorities. Important findings:

1. The group leaders were invited (a) the group who had been in the UK more than 20 years (b) general group (c) 'Nazis'. The demand from group (a) and (b) is to be separated from group (c). Lord Lytton questioned Gunter from group c regarding his attitude to England and Germany and his position regarding groups (a) and (b). He replied in a stupid way that his group was as loyal to England as Germany, whereupon Lord L cut short further contribution with the remark that he now had sufficient information.

2. We could not count on being liberated soon. There were plans for those released to be given an international pass – like the Nansen pass[104] after

the First World War, which entitled the bearer to be given protection against any further persecution, exclusive of prosecution by the Nazi countries.

3. Improvement to medical care
4. Agreeing to the speeding up of the postal services
5. Measures to be taken during an air raid.

This morning I wanted to demonstrate a few exercises to Dr Waldheim – Gustav and Piner joined us – I am going to do some exercises early every morning.

13 August 1940

Yesterday afternoon a lecture by Professor S. on an 'Introduction to philosophy'. He is a first-class speaker with 30 years' experience as a lecturer. He is, of course, convinced that only philosophy can save society – he rejected sharply all, as I call them, 'potato philosophers' – amateurs, people who are ignorant, who say that they devise their own philosophy, through personal experiences and reject the speculations of the 'experts'. The prerequisite of any philosopher is for him to have mastered a branch of knowledge; Plato and Aristotle built on mathematical knowledge, Socrates on questioning, Nietzsche on philology. In my opinion every true believer – i.e. people who live passionately and committed with complete honesty according to their convictions – leads a good life. Their material life will no doubt be driven by circumstances but whatever life events they encounter, their internal life will not be changed.

In the evening I attended a Jewish service in Hut 8, a service of Tischeb'av (mourning), a service for the remembrance of the destruction of Jerusalem. It was a rational/religious service, an orthodox cantor led the monotonous sing-song of the mourning prayer sitting on a low stool (a symbol, you collapse under the burden of sorrow and throw yourself onto mother earth). In the light of a candle, which is a reminder of childhood, I recall the devout sitting Shiva in the main synagogue, which was decked out in black with the prayer desk covered in a black cloth with silver embroidery, the wonderful mourning litanies. I recollect that I was the disembodied solo singer at the service. By the end of the service, grasping the hand of my father, I felt that I had given him great pleasure. And at his side was Rabbi Lamel, a 70 year-old, our neighbour who said to him that I had never sang so well. I couldn't help myself, I cried as I did at my mother's death and I feel how the hand of my father grasps my hand and nothing more was said. And I remember my grandmother too who spent her days dressed in dark colours and in deep mourning. It would be a loss if all this were to disappear from the world. I believe God's word: 'they were, they are and they will be in order to spread the fame of Jehovah for all time' – with which I end the mourning service in my own way.

My fellow house sharer, Ing Holz, who opened a factory with Wolfram contacts (a competitor of Bosch) has suddenly been released, good chap. Gustav Schönberg received a telegram, Martin is arriving on Wednesday, hopefully I will see him. Dachinger has made a third coloured sketch of me, I think the best yet. He says he is beginning to know me now that he has discovered my intellectual head and I, simple fool, have discovered it too.

14 August 1940

I handed Gustav Schönberg the questionnaire to give to Martin and also the letter to Onkel Gustl, and a request for a dustpan and broom. I was at Dr Jacobson's. A new examination is scheduled with the English doctor. I am to ask the 'house father' to put my name down on the invalid list. Actually all this is a bit of a swizz. There are so many really sick people (those with TB, those with angina, half blind) who are not being released. Thus if it were a matter of justice, I would remain here until the miserable plebs get to release the oldies. Never! The authorities are not on the side of the angels. Yesterday an Australian plane crashed in the vicinity of Melbourne, killing the general staff, the defence, war and foreign affairs Ministers who were travelling to Melbourne for a meeting.[105] As my mother always said: 'Who knows why things happen?' Mittler posted a note on our front door a few days ago, how naïve, inviting people to come to his lecture about three-dimensional geometry. Pedant that he is, under the invitation he left space for people to register with their surnames, first name, number and address – of course no one put their name down. This morning after breakfast, while washing up, Karl and I wrote six joke names on it, and right at the end Karl wrote my name – great hilarity – even Mittler was amused.

15 August 1940

Martin was here for two hours yesterday and spoke with Gustav Sch. On his departure I was only able to speak with him for a minute and press his hand. He said the Durgans are furious and he will do his best to send a request for release with the medical certificate. Gustav gave him a request, together with the letter to Onkel Gustl, asking for a broom and a dustpan. Thank God he looks very well. He found taking leave of his brother Robert[106] very hard. Martin only wants to emigrate if there is no other possibility. I was at an artistic amateur talent competition this evening. The best poem was by Dr Steindler. I am going to try and get hold of them. Also a serious poem by a certain D. and good English poems by a young refugee who apparently has been living here for 33 years. Otherwise the highlight was the performances by the singers – two older singers. In the middle of the event there was an air-raid alarm, 99% of the audience remained in their seats, the warning sirens no longer affect people. Getting used to daily night air-raids lulls people into a sense that there is no danger- how unaware of fear they have become – how they would panic if a bomb were really to fall. Gottfurcht has put me down on the invalid list. In the afternoon Karl and I waited at Gustav's to be summoned by Martin B., had black coffee with shortbread. This Dr Weissenberg is an empathetic chap, he is particularly sympathetic despite his great knowledge and deep piety. He was active in Berlin for years in the organisation of religious socialists. He takes the fundamentalist teaching of Jesus as a given. Characteristically, I showed him the poem by W. and said I would like to show it to Gustav, whereupon he retorted 'Don't do that, let him pull himself together' – how very decent.

16 August 1940

Three air-raid alarms tonight, I was not particularly disturbed. I think I only woke up properly at the third, probably through the rummaging and tramping around of Mittler, who came to see me last night at 10:00 in order to inform me what a great fellow he was. In a single afternoon – listen and wonder – he had set up (and organised) all the air-raid staff and his brain is brimming with good deeds. He sees himself as the saviour of the camp, he agrees enthusiastically with my remark that the possibility of a bomb falling on our camp is 1:100,000,[107] which does not stop him, most conscientiously before he goes to sleep every evening, opening the taps in the bath so there is water in the case of fire and telling Karl who is always the last in the bathroom 'please can he turn off the taps when he finishes'. This pleases Austerlitz greatly because next morning he can bathe in the water that has been stored. Which all goes to prove that even the greatest nonsense can be useful in the end.

I listened to Brahms's second symphony on the Camp radio and went to the coffee house to meet Professor Witbek, Gustav and four more 'intellectuals'. Witbek mocked, most amusingly, the afternoon lecture by Dr A. about Kabbalistic number symbolism which led to a good debate about Jews. Witbek has sent a telegram to apply for an appointment at the Archaeological Institute in New York. He was the founder and head of the German Institute in Constantinople. After Hitler came to power, he went to Brussels, taught for five years, fled from the Germans, arrived in England with the English troops from Dunkirk, destitute, with only one suit and without any documents.

Wrote to Hansl. Sent on the letter to Dr Mayer from his mother with our greetings. Skipped gym today. Gustav Sch was unwell in the night. Stomach cramps and diarrhoea. Dr A. and Dr W. saw to him and he was better in the morning.

17 August 1940

Was at Schönberg's in the afternoon. Dr A had organised a tea party, the so-called meal was only a cheese sandwich with some tea. I then read a little. But I indulged myself when I got home: in a tin of herrings in tomato sauce with bread and margarine, between the three of us. Each of us had a bottle of beer and then a cigar from Martin. Felt like a Lord, smoking a cigar, lying in bed reading, savouring it. In the afternoon at Schönberg's, got to know a Dr Frankfürter; he turns out to be a grandson of 'Wichlau' Frankfürter from Nikolsburg, the brother-in-law of Rabbi Lamel, our neighbour in Nikolsburg. He is a self-made man and he brought back old memories and was a good raconteur of Jewish jokes. In the morning had a good game of bridge in our room. Gustav received a letter from Martin and Grete which crossed with a letter of the 3 August. Grete had not yet got my acknowledgement of her letters and the contents, I shall send it today. Tonight there was no air-raid and I slept throughout uninterrupted. The English report that they shot down 167 out of the 1,000 German planes over the UK yesterday, over the last 4 days they have shot down more than 450: if this is true, it would be good.[108] I cannot visualise how a conquest of England could be done by air – unless they were to send thousands, flooding the air with bombs, but even then it seems impossible. They cannot destroy the whole country with bombs that have only single impact but it is all too unimaginably horrific. Thinking about it could drive one to suicide, nearly out of one's mind – putting your head in the sand politics. Karl is doing his exercises with his gas mask on but no clothes on the upper part of his body, it's a sight for sore eyes.

10:30pm

A letter from Hansl with two affidavits for me, so things are hotting up. Registered letter from Martin with £5 posted on the 12th, really kind. From Mrs Constant, a friend of Dr Mayer's, a very nice reply to my letter, she is a twenty four year old young woman, must be quite lively, I'm to tell her what I need, offering to send me books, food etc.

18 August 1940

A satisfactory day. While washing up, had a set to with Colonel Mittler, he came to see me in the scullery feeling guilty. I am standing at the sink, he tries to push past me, he says he has no time, he is very busy. I tell him to go out by the other exit. At the second attempt I bar his way. The idiot says he can't get by me, I shove him away, whereupon he exclaims in a temper: 'that would just suit you, were the house to be bombed, it would be me that pulled you out to safety'. The comedy of the situation overcomes me, I respond laughing uncontrollably: 'My dear chap, the first one to get out will be you as you are always pushing your way to the front'. Early in the morning E. drags me into his room in order to ask my advice, in his touching way, regarding his twelve year-old daughter, who is being well looked after, until she is eighteen, whilst he moves to the USA. He asks my advice about whether he should leave her behind – he is afraid of estrangement and his influence being weakened. I advise him, giving my reasons, to leave her here. Towards the end of our conversation Mittler rushes in – I'm just smoking one of Martin's excellent cigarettes – I only smoke one a week. Despite the open window Mittler remarks: 'the air in my room is being polluted, you are introducing bacteria, at the most you will live a fifth less than non-smokers.' The conversation is at an end.

In the evening there was a concert in Hut1: Beethoven, Waldheim Sonata; Schubert; Chopin; and E minor sonata by Brahms for piano and cello. In the afternoon a lecture by Weissenberg on 'the new physics' – popular but not comprehensible for the layman, nor for me – obviously due to my lack of mathematical knowledge, I cannot visualise five-dimensional calculations. W. says you should not try to imagine, but should just calculate. There are apparently 140 proofs of the Pythagoras theorem.

19 August 1940

Sunday, totally washed out: things are very bad in poor weather – the worst is that you sink into the mud and your shoes stay stuck in the wet clay floor.

You come into the house with straw-covered shoes and you have nothing to clean yourself up with – corridors, rooms, mud everywhere and getting worse and worse. Went for a walk with Dr F. a good friend of Dr R., we have many acquaintances in common. He and his brother are going to the Isle of Man tomorrow with about another eighty people, also Ing Kalisch who is now interned in his fifth camp. Ernst Kerner is now released, he is leaving tomorrow morning. People are constantly coming and going.

Hansl is in constant communication with the Uncle of Hans Oppenheimer, Julius Oppenheimer.[109] Uncle Julius receives two or three business telegrams from Hans Oppenheimer a week and says without doubt everything is fine with them in Alexandria. Yesterday was Kaiser Franz Joseph's birthday – what festivities there were on this day before the war! All swept away, we are in a ghost world – unbelievable. People had no worries, were cheerful, enjoyed their lives – and now? One wakes up full of anxieties and you go to bed with the thought, 'what will the night bring?' I feel for the miseries of the whole of mankind – two air-raids last night, in the afternoon two air battles over London, eighty-seven German planes shot down. You listen to the radio and think of all the young lives lost, of the German bombs…

20 August 1940

An air-mail letter from my sister Ida, posted 6 July. So far all is well – but she is very sad – she has not received any post – she clings with touching love to her memories, to the day of Marc's death, various birthdays. Unfortunately she still has pains in her hands and is not any better. Fritz could keep in contact but seems to be indifferent. Yesterday, I received two parcels from Martin: six tins of sausages; one chicken – particularly good, gave half to Schönberg; four tins of sausages which we will store. A 'poetic evening' with recitals from the poets, 'works' created in the camp, said to be lyrics. Those that read were: Fritz Gross, Krammers, Lüstig (bad), Drücker (middling), H (good), Dr Zauber(very good). I think they are all Austrian – Viennese. In the afternoon, a game of bridge at our place. If it is true that your character shows itself under the influence of alcohol or playing cards, then Karl is a dick-head. The main difference between us: for me the game is for amusement or distraction, for him it is serious knowledge – perhaps he is right? By the way, yesterday I made the discovery to my astonishment that the crockery for twelve people is washed three times daily, with a rag thirty centimetres square and another rag six centimetres square. These rags have never been washed since my arrival on the 29 June. They are gunged up with fat. You can guess how our joint tin of cutlery gets to be 'clean' – everything is covered with a film of margarine and there is never any hot water. But then – one could also say – who knows what makes you ill. Two air-raids: at 11:00 and 3:00 with heavy bombardment at the latter time. They do not bother me in the least any more, I wake and then fall asleep in a little while, wrapped in the sound of the sirens, which sound like music to me.

21 August 1940

Another airmail card from Ida from15 July, pretty good. She has apparently received some of my letters from June but she has not yet been informed about my internment. They live very quietly on Mount Carmel, they don't even hear the sirens during air-raids. Postal connections in Palestine are being tightened, parcels containing letters are destroyed, special letters and telegrams are reduced to the most urgent. Yesterday I was invited for an evening meal at Dr A., frankfurters with potatoes and cheese, cigars. After which I went for a walk and conversation with Dr P. who told me various interesting things about his flight from Vienna, how he got out jewellery, furs etc. He was the first person to get his PhD under the Nazi regime – his 15 years of study were interrupted.

Martin over-feeds us with food parcels – a whole box of tins arrived for me and Gustav. I received a small parcel of sausages and a small tin without a label to identify the sender. Karl got a parcel with bacon, Linzer torte and walnut cake. I told F. that I'm withdrawing my application to leave, we're so well cared for here! Franzl G. visited me. He wants to be moved, he is in the same room as a fanatical mixed-race person who sees himself as a Nazi. He has spoken with Dr Waldheim and Gustav to request the bunk of Dr A.

Dachinger made the fourth sketch of me today, sitting, the whole upper body. The head, in my opinion, is the most successful yet. He gave me a sample of a beautifully created invitation by him and Rosen to their art exhibition and invited me for Friday to a sausage feast.

I got to know Dr Ehrenberg, a Protestant vicar of Jewish origin, formerly a professor in Heidelberg. His grandfather from Vienna, by the name of Finkl, wrote a book in the 1870s, called 'German Water Legislation'. Sent a letter to Gustidl and Joyce Constant (the woman who offered to send parcels) yesterday. There are more and more cats and dogs on the camp, where do people find them? Yesterday morning, I listened at the window of Dr A's. to the Schubert quintet; on the bed sits a charming ginger/white, at most four weeks old, kitten, listening too. No doubt, the longing for pets is a consequence of the need for love and surely a form of eroticism. It is good to observe this need in our dormitory – colleague Austerlitz has brought up a cat, now five years old; his face lights up when he talks about the animal. He, the quiet one, becomes chatty and doesn't tire of telling us how she sits for hours by his side without moving, while he is drawing, and looks at him with her great green eyes, steadfastly. As soon as he packs up his drawing tools and sits down she jumps onto his lap, begins to purr, slides up his stomach and with her velvety paws caresses his cheeks. He has given the creature to simple folk to look after who report weekly (and get well paid for this). The man is a foreman in a factory, and the woman a housewife and they report as follows; couple sitting at breakfast, the cat suddenly becomes restless, jumps onto the lap of the woman, then goes to the door, does this repeatedly so that the couple go to the front room to see what is going on, they find a letter from Austerlitz on the floor, a letter which they would only have found hours afterwards – strange.

22 August 1940

Yesterday from 8:00 to 10:30 a seminar by Dr E. on Nietzsche, 'The will to power', the first time I have participated in a philosophical seminar. Those that took part in the discussion were Professor Weissenberg, Dr Frisch, and Unger; this is how I imagine the Talmudic schools analyse and explain texts. Tomorrow evening Dr Unger is going to talk about critical theory. I actually wanted to intervene, I was curious to ascertain how a technical brain compares to a speculative thinker in becoming a future philosopher. We technical people are forced to express our thoughts in constructions, in will and deeds and therefore offer a practical approach in comparison to metaphysical philosophers; for example Popper-Lynkeus's and his 'general nutritional obligation'.[110]

Dr M. from Bromley has gone, similarly Dr Samuel received a telegram informing him of his release. Dr Samuel will ask Dr Bach to give Martin an official report on my health which should then be sent on to the camp father. Today on the parade ground there was a short leave taking for Dr Weissenberg, who left the camp in the afternoon; these events were formerly done with a lot of ceremony. His replacement is Dr Elkan. Earlier at the roll call held by the refugees, I laughed heartily; a civil servant from the Home Office in Coy had a hobby horse thrust between his legs; it was a sight fit to be photographed.

10:00pm

Today at six o'clock in the evening, I was lying on my bed reading and Karl storms in and says that I am to be released. I thought he was joking – whereupon he assured me of the truth of his information. Dr A. had passed it on to him. Sir John Anderson had today declared in Parliament that the age of internees is to be reduced from 70 to 65.[111] As always happens when I am surprised by some major event, my feelings overwhelmed me and I began to cry. Suddenly I recognised my own and everyone's misery, the whole charade of jolliness which I act when people are around, collapsed suddenly and I stood there naked – it was a shame that I was not alone. In the evening at Gustav's, Dr A., Dr Ing F., Dr Waldstein and I ate sausages with sauerkraut, rollmops, biscuits, beer – joined by Dr F. who also announced his imminent release and repeated the same jokes he told us 5 days ago resulting in '*nebbisch*'[112] and a little senility. Trotsky has been knocked down with a rake brought in clandestinely by a certain Jackson – Anglicised name of an immigrant Russian – (Jew?) and injured so badly that he was not allowed to get up. So the career of one of the most significant revolutionaries, the best colleague of Lenin's and the creator of the Soviet Army has been brought to an end.[113] He was a noble Jew, in the category of 'Jesus' Jews.

23 August 1940

Slept through – I was exhausted – to 6:00am and woke with bad headache. Took two aspirins – nothing helped – now it is 9:30 and I'm feeling better – obviously it is all to do with nerves. Went to see Doctor T. as first patient for my welfare – we made a bet that I would be out by the 31st otherwise he has lost the bet. Today I was at the gym – terrible weather, stormy, rain. Charming letter from Ida Kerner, enchanting both in its content and style; nice letter from Gustl Bunzl – the sender of the small packets, Gustav seems to have announced to the whole world that the 'gymnastics' are a great event- Gustl Bunzl mentions it and reminds me of when we jointly did gymnastics in the Langegasse. I can't stop thinking about Franz Tedesco. I hope to God that my presentiments are false. Last bridge party with the Freund brothers who are leaving for the Isle of Man today.

Continued 10:00pm

Dinner, as a guest of the painter Dachinger, with Gustav, Karl, Austerlitz and myself. Sausages, bacon, nut cake, coffee, cigars. At 8:00pm they came to get Gustav to go to the camp authorities – he is released and is going home tomorrow lunch time. I was with him till a few minutes ago. Dr Waldheim recounts authentically, that there is a diabetic in the camp who has opened a shop with a delivery service – he delivers his urine, for which he gets paid good money, to healthy people who then get released as diabetics. His business is flourishing – Oh these Israelites! What other race would have this 'Judas' thought? Gustav left at noon. Dr A. at 10:00am. I am accompanied to the parade ground by Dr Waldheim and Dr A. who arrived yesterday evening at 11:30pm from Sutton Coldfield camp. He was badly treated there and had to sleep on bare earth for eighteen days. Our camp was designed to provide housing for workers, it was supposed to replace the Liverpool slums. It is very practically-built housing, exceptionally cheap, with every square metre utilised as on a ship. Yet it provides a good living environment, each house has a flushing WC, a bathroom and warm water. Every two houses have a 0.8m wide alleyway between them, roofed over so that there is a covered link between all the streets. There is plenty of fresh air, a space for gardens at the front and back.

24 August 1940

Below is a sketch of our house – typical of all of them. In the main streets they also have attic rooms, somewhat larger houses and a second WC on the first floor.

The walls and floors are paper thin; the doors and windows are a botched job – the cheapest iron cladding, gaps everywhere, always open to west and north-west winds. You only have to look at the ground plan to realise that, when the ground floor doors A, B, and C are open, the whole house acts like a chimney stack. The draught goes through despite the closed door so that our washing, hung over our bunks, flaps in the wind. Austerlitz has erected a great cardboard lid at his feet (where has he stolen it from?) so that he is not blown away. Even on still days the corridor doors bang shut with the wind, as most of the occupants can't manage to hold the door in their hand and close them gently. The whole house resounds as though with canon shots – one would think that the whole house of cards would collapse. Whilst I am writing, at intervals of several minutes, there is always a Boom! Boom! And I have to interrupt my writing because the table, which serves the whole house and is carried backwards and forwards, wobbles. It has got to the point that the table comes into our room after roll call when I yell, 'Table, all change!'

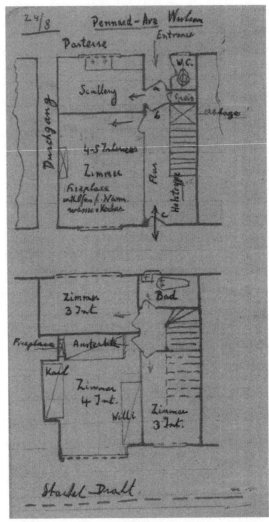

Detailed Drawing of Pennard Avenue flats. Wilhelm Hollitscher's diary, 24 August 1940. Wiener Library

Key to drawing

Ground Floor: Durchgang= passage way, Entrance, WC, Scullery, Zimmer= room for 4-5 internees, Fireplace mit ofen warm wasser & kocken = fireplace with oven, warm water and cooker, Flur = floor, Holztreppe = wooden staircase, Aplage = storage

Upstairs: 3 bedrooms and a bath. Two of the bedroom are for 3 internees. The one at the bottom left says it is for 4 internees but Wilhelm only shows 3 beds- his bed (Willi), Karl's bed and Austerlitz's bed. It is possible that Gustav Schönberg had the fourth bed but Wilhelm mentions on the 22 July that Gustav was moved to the special diet hostel and he might not have been replaced.

Bottom: Stachel Draht = Barbed Wire

Last night, after an interlude of 3 days, there was another air-raid. I observed it lying in bed, the sky full of search lights, droning of planes, but no bombs. Good letter from Gerti [niece],[114] she had passed the second interview panel, she has permission to work again in a hospital. Karl and Anny together with the Schlesingers and Stella in Montaubon, 30 kilometres north of Toulouse, are trying to get an affidavit through the Laufers who are in New York.

26 August 1940

Yesterday Sunday, at 7 in the evening, Polatschek comes and congratulates me, saying that I am to be released today; yesterday was two months since my arrest. One cannot trust his assurances, yet we organised a small celebratory leave-taking meal, Karl, Austerlitz, Mittler, Polatschek and I – bacon, salmon, cake and compote. We all engaged in an interesting conversation – with the exception of Mittler, who always, more and more, shows himself to be 'an old Viennese' with limited natural intelligence – but otherwise quite inoffensive. Dachinger presented me with his latest sketch of me which is generally approved as good – a nice memento. My nerves are very much on edge (I am trembling inwardly) – of course, I do not show my agitation. The crazy tragedy of our fate; additionally the thought that this will not be the last adventure of my earthly existence, which so longs for peace and quiet. They hound you, they plague you, and they torment you until they draw blood through the mud with this yellow insignia, Jew, Jew, Jew. I read today that Hitler has annexed conquered Poland into his Reich. He has divided it into four districts, Cracow, Warsaw, Lublin and Radom and all the Jews are confined to ghettos, identifiable in towns through white arm bands with a Star of David. So we are back to where we were 500 years ago – finally the ghetto is the only means for the survival of our kind.[115]

27 August 1940

Nothing has transpired – Gottfurcht thinks it might take 14 days. Yesterday evening in Hut 10, there was a leave-taking evening for Wiener, who has left the camp today, which was entitled 'Old Austria and Vienna'. They sang a special Viennese song, a Schubert song, and old Viennese popular songs with a small choir – it was pleasant. In the afternoon I was at a bridge party at Ollendorf's, 5 of us, he is the only Viennese, a 'lousy' lot. Then the 'super' group, Karl, Austerlitz and myself, cooked up tinned food in the kitchen: bacon, cake and beer. On release, I shall have to get used again to my simple life. I am living most luxuriously and indulging; Karl and Austerlitz each had a cigar- I've still got 3.

I spent the afternoon with Dachinger, he is a good guy. We chatted about his work, it is great how he paints a picture. Ended with a sing song with some good choruses. We internees are the 'free ones', the captured ones are the soldiers and the officers. It all depends on how the spirit rises above the circumstances. I have borrowed the song words from Relly as follows:
Full text follows of:

I.   My Bonnie lies over the ocean.
II.   The night has gone, The golden sun,Shines over the sea and land, Oh Father love, Oh God above, Take me gently by the hand.
III. Pack up your troubles in your old kit-bag.
IV.   Sleep, baby, sleep.
V.   Old Lang Syne.
VI.   Clementine.
VII. Loch Lomond.

Kremers entertained us this morning with the good-humoured wit with which he teased Mittler.We are all assembled at the roll call, he is the last one to join us and he says with a glint in his eye 'Oh the devil, the devil, what is going on? Something has got to give: our boss, the air raid warden, can't sleep, starts up in the night although for the last two days there has been no air-raid alarm. He is thinking of handing in his notice as there is no profit in all his work, after all he gets a percentage on every air-raid' – and more in this vein to the amusement of the entire company. Wrote to Richard. Still no news about Franz Tedesco. Inexplicable – perhaps it is only bad postal communication. Outgoing letters take between one and three weeks to get to London. Captain Smith, with whom Kremers spoke after roll call this morning, said he was quite right, his complaint was fully justified. He had spoken to the Camp Commandant who had written a sharp letter to the censor, he could not do more.

The English lesson at Blumenfeld's was good. If only I could pull myself together and be more studious, I would manage to reach a good intermediate standard in English. In the morning at the English class I met Doring, an interesting chap. He is amusing and lets people sing English folk songs (above) at the end of the lesson.

28 August 1940

A postscript to Kremers's utterances – the business with the air raids, he claims they are a Jewish invention, they go back to ancient Egypt when the Jews migrated to 'air-raids' (erez) Israel.[116] Yesterday the first evening air-raid was at 10:30pm. Kremers and others read me Hamlet in English. I followed with the help of a translation. It was very good, Kremers reads extremely well. In the afternoon I had an English lesson atBlumenfeld's. After tea went to Fischer's where I participated in a real dinner including: an egg dish – something I've not eaten for months, salami, cheese and continental bread. Then we went to the 'pub'. We each had a bottle of beer. Went for a walk, nine o'clock news. Hanna Bunzl is coming on Saturday. Fischer is thinking of telegramming her to put her off, I think this was only a pose, he wanted to make himself interesting. The absence of any news about Franz Tedesco makes me think the worst. I hope to God that my premonitions are wrong.

29 August 1940

Telegram from Martin. Franz is well. I should not send the affidavit to the consulate, they look forward to my arrival. A high official from the Home Office, a member of the Advisory Council, was here yesterday, actually it was only a weak blackmail attempt to persuade those aged between 18 and 50 to join the Pioneer Corps. Received a fairly cool take up despite his announcement that the general internment policy is not being altered. All those over 65 must renew their application for release again, I handed mine in early this morning. Dr Waldheim says the Commandant is doing his best to speed matters up and to reduce the size of the camp.

For the occasion of the 191st birthday of Goethe, there was a Goethe festival in Hut 1. An introduction by a string quartet who played the Andante by Haydn in E flat, then the prologue to Faust with various roles – both pretty mediocre. The main speech in honour of Goethe was by Siebert – a whole lot of waffle – I left. You wouldn't think it possible that an experienced professor of philosophy could utter such platitudes.In the evening, I was in Gustav's room with Dr T., Waldheim, Fischer, and Dr A. for a beer evening. I shall find it hard in Petts Wood to give up this idle existence. The night was very disturbed: planes, bombs exploding, the last one very close, they say one landed behind the football pitch and two soldiers were wounded. From my bed I could see the sky lit up with search lights, I heard the droning of the bombs and the explosions, nevertheless I fell gently asleep.

30 August 1940

Yesterday afternoon there was the opening of the exhibition, '*Art behind the Wire*', in a new corrugated iron shed. Professor Hamburger gave the opening speech explaining the concept. The Colonel responded. I had been invited by Dachinger. The presentation of the pictures was excellent with paper screens – sections – obviously in the camp these were primitive measures. Dachinger has his own small room. My picture and Kramers's and his mood sketches – everything on newspaper – much in pencil, charcoal, pastels and water colour. Some very good portraits of A., D. and Sch. Very witty caricatures of Rot, Müller, Baier. Rosen has made a placard entitled '*War means only Peace*', on newspaper with water colours, the British Lion in an aggressive pose pressing down on German planes with his front paw; and a fantastic caricature called '*Censor's Constipation*', a naked overweight man sitting on a pot. A lot of people say that Dachinger is the best and most talented. Very witty pen drawings, caricatures by Ing. Huber, Karl bought one. Conversation as follows: Karl goes to the seller who has overpriced the caricature and asks if he can have a reproduction; reply 'you know he is such a lazy dog he wouldn't do it twice'. When Karl agrees to the original price of one shilling, Huber says 'I'm the lazy dog'. Huber comes from E. I asked him about the Laufers who are relatives.

In the evening I was with Karl in the newly-opened small bar, each of us drank a bottle of ale. At 10:30 there was an air-raid which lasted until 3:00am, heavy bomb explosions so near that the houses shook. Karl is to be envied, despite continuous bombing and heavy defensive flak, he fell asleep and without waking, snored until 7:30 in the morning. But I too fell asleep towards midnight and didn't hear anything more, although I woke with a bad headache. An unpleasant scene between Kramers and me, on the one side and Mittler on the other side. We were standing in a hallway when Mittler comes and tells us we should go to bed. When we refused he broke into an hysterical fit of rage and yelled out obscenities. I advised him to go to bed and get psychiatric treatment. He is a bad-tempered, simpleton, 'cultured' oaf. Kramers, who has known him for 30 years, mediated and reproached me with the inappropriateness of my remarks, and advised him to overcome his pride. The English can't abide such an hysterical Jew.

Sensation of the day: Schapinger has come back from hospital and looks pretty good. A letter (airmail) from Lisl from 19/07 – already old news. The contents are quite good; Hans writes that Hannele and Lisl are blooming. Hans hasn't heard anything from his sister and brother-in-law for six months. I have to repeat my application for release because I made an error in filling it in.

Released on 31 August 1940

I was called to Captain Thomas early at 10:30am – sent home, small error, recalled 20 minutes later to Dr Wolput – sent home again – medical was positive. Wolput's report still has to be signed by the Commandant. I am waiting, with 90% probability that I'll be in Petts Wood tomorrow evening – at home – (in a foreign place). It's a lucky coincidence that I received the letter from Lisl and Hans yesterday. They had received my letters from the 18 and 25 June on the day they wrote.

Played bridge yesterday afternoon and evening with Professor Lang. Because the dispatch of his documents from Blomsbury House in Liverpool was delayed, he was taken off the ship and was transported here for some days. Thus one meets again with people who re-emerge on the scene. As an epilogue to my stay I am writing back at my Hut. To bed at 10:30. 10:45 put out the light. At 11:30 an air-raid alarm which I didn't hear – slept through it. Austerlitz was up till 3:00am, disturbed by the night bombs and flak defences, even Karl came up. I don't hear anything anymore, may it be and continue so.

Tonight, a leave-taking supper at Fischer's with Karl and Dr Waldheim who told me (OK – I admit my silly vanity has emerged again) that I was the greatest attraction of his stay. He regarded it as a small blessing sent by God and these small blessings are actually the ones to be most valued. He asked me to visit his wife and to invite myself for lunch – she would be pleased to be able to cook well for me. Even though he is a flatterer and many of his words are not to be taken at face value, still the matter pleased me greatly. It is sufficient if there is a bit of truth in it and, in any case, it reflects well on him. I was fetched in the afternoon, received my documents – I'm released – I'm travelling at 12:45 tomorrow to Liverpool. At 9:30am I'm to withdraw my money from Captain Fiedler- an end to the Huyton-days. Karl made a good joke this morning to reinforce a remark that he made that was disputed – 'I swear by the holy Huyton that it is true`.

Petts Wood, 2 September 1940

I took my leave of Huyton yesterday on Sunday afternoon. I received various goodbye visits, several people requested that I intervene on their behalf outside or go to Embassies. I was seen off by various internees, especially Dr Waldheim, who asked as a particular favour whether he could carry my case to the meeting place in hut 21 where we got our railway tickets and the Commandant made a brief leave-taking speech. Back in my Hut, I had an intimate breakfast with Karl, Kramers and Austerlitz. Then I went to Liverpool by bus where I tried in vain to telephone and was also unable to send a telegram. Left Liverpool at 2:10, arrived in Euston with some delay at 7:10. Travelled in the company of Block, Eisenmann and Brin, very pious German Jews, who spent much of the journey reading Jewish magazines and praying. After some difficulty I found a taxi (not before, laden with my luggage, I fell over a case standing in my way) to Charing Cross, caught the 7:34 train to Petts Wood. Arrived home around 9:15pm. I had an enthusiastic welcome from all the Durgans, the most enthusiastic being Todge – with whom I celebrated a moving reunion. The Durgans immediately informed Ida Kerner, who herself informed Martin and in no time we were all assembled. Herbert[117] appeared with a bottle of good wine. The joy of the welcome was fantastic. Then our hunger having being satisfied, Lili Bunzl and Lisl came. Got to bed at 10:30.

This morning a short visit to the four ladies' house,[118] then to Franz and Nelly Weiss where I reported fully on Karl. Then to London to Onkel Gustl where my heart opened up. I can report 'kisses' from no fewer than seven women, all of them platonic. From Onkel Gustl, I went back to Orpington to report to the police. The Durgans have re-papered my small room, beautifully done up. I get the feeling that I have been welcomed like a child of the family and so nothing remains to be done but to thank God for all the good things that I have experienced in the last ten weeks.

Epilogue

I was therefore interned from the 25 June to the 1 September. Views about the background to these events fall into two categories. Some claim it was the result of the atmosphere of panic; the Government having lost its head after the collapse of France. Others say it was simply the fault of the 'military machine'. The military chose the path of least resistance and they sacrificed the 'refugees'. From my a-political standpoint I have avoided taking part in such discussions. I myself believe and fear that Fascism reaches up into the highest circles. I also believe that there exists an antisemitic alternative government, supported by members of the governing classes, which has its own views and is active and sabotages members of the government with a different view. One can see evidence in the articles that were published (particularly against Wells, Wedgewood, Rusholme[119]) and I have personal knowledge of the case of Gottfurcht, a typical example of sabotage. However, the incarceration of a few thousand Austrian and German Jews and 10% Aryans is not so bad. Much more dangerous is the fact that many, because they are Czech citizens or Hungarian, are able to run about freely and can do what they want despite being part of the Axis. However, all this is gossip – we are stumbling around in the dark and can do nothing but let what is going to happen become more imminent: as the English say: 'wait and see'.

It is all nonsense: anyway, I have benefitted from these last two months which for me have been a valuable lesson in goodness and decency as well as a stimulating adventure which I consider an enrichment of my twilight years. I asked many about their impressions in Dachau and Buchenwald, to describe the difference between the British and German experience – strange – the majority did not report on the moral and spiritual side. The only thing they emphasised was their own well-being. The Germans had organised the whole thing in an excellent way. You had beds there, sheets, tables, chairs everything worked perfectly, even the food, although scarce, was better. When it came to their treatment, they said it had not been so bad. Some, who were not adaptable, had had bad experiences. But people forget so quickly; it is the same phenomenon as a bad illness which disappears from your memory. In fact I have actually forgotten what I suffered and could only reconstruct my operation and suffering through my writings.

Apart from satisfying my sense of adventure, which at my age is something, I have got to know some fantastic people. Thanks to my innate positive attitude, I was able to give encouragement to those who were feeling depressed. But what will remain with me for the rest of my life is the knowlege of friendship and love, the attachment and warmth of all Petts Woodians. So it is in life: it is only when one falls into distress and needs help,(which didn't fully happen in my case) that real friendship reveals itself. They were <u>ALL </u>(as an aside, Martin in the first place – how could it be otherwise?) touchingly kind to me. So I came back with a feeling that I was back home again. I'm among good empathetic friends to whom, as long as I live, I shall continue to be grateful.It is exactly this feeling of solidarity that will make a decision to join Hansl so difficult, even if it is a distant decision. The time spent here and in the camp has not been in vain, I count it as a positive in my time on earth.

Yesterday afternoon, I wrote various letters for those still interned. There were three air-raids, the last 10:30 at night, fell asleep, heard the all clear. The Germans are making a damned effort, the island is besieged. Hopefully they have taken on more than they can chew. In the meantime, the Germans and Italians have taken two-thirds of Transylvania from the Romanians.[120] So Romania is today exactly as it was in 1914, everything that they stole 'honestly' has been taken from them again.

Martin came to an agreement with Mr Durgan during my absence, the rent 1 shilling a day was paid to the 01/09. Martin gave me accounts with some financial support for July and August. I managed to retain £5 5 shillings. My credit at Lloyds Bank altogether £64 14 shillings and 2 pence.

I telegrammed Gustidl, will try to send Gustav some money to Palestine. I will telegraph Hansl today to tell him I'm free.

Notes

1   Ida (1877-1942) was Wilhelm's sister and brought up Lisl (his daughter), as Marianne, his wife, had depression. Gustav was also a Hollitscher but not a blood relative of Ida and Wilhelm. Ida and Wilhelm were very close. The Gustildls left Vienna after Wilhelm and went to Palestine on 31 November 1939.

2   Marc Hollitscher (1869-1910), Wilhelm's brother, went to Gablonz in the Czech Republic as a 'koncipient'(articled lawyer) and in 1901 he came home, married, and established himself as a fully qualified lawyer in Vienna, both in the Court of Law and at the Royal Court. He rescued the family from their period of material deprivation which had dominated since their move to Vienna in 1886. Only one his children and two of his step grandchildren survived the war.

3   Marie (Mini) Hollitscher (1871-1934). She was a primary school teacher and never married.

4   Now known as Mikulov in the Czech Republic.

5   Gustav (1861-1941). Hollitscher referred to with his wife Ida as Gustidl. Gustav was also a Hollitscher but not a blood relative of Ida and Wilhelm. The Gustildls left Vienna after Wilhelm and went to Palestine on 31 November 1939.

6   Hans (Hansl) Hollitscher (1911-1992), Wilhelm's son, left Vienna before his father to establish a home and got a paint spaying job in Salford. He left for the USA at the end of 1939 and in January 1940 was sent to Cselalis, two and a half hour bus journey from Seattle, under a resettlement scheme. After the war he became a bookkeeper in Seattle moving to San Francisco in 1965 as a civil service accountant. He was an active member of the Sierra Club, doing voluntary work for them when he retired. He never married nor had children.

7   Stella Laufer (1894-194?) She was the daughter of Wilhelm's sister, Hanna Laufer, She and her brother Paul Laufer were victims of the Holocaust.

8   Fritz Hollitscher (1891-1944). Simon (Wilhelm's father) describes him as follows in 1917: 'There was a man called David Kohn, a bookkeeper whose family lived in the same corridor as ourselves. He and his wife, who were not particularly well-off, died very quickly one after the other in the space of a few weeks, leaving behind five children at a very tender and sensitive age. We, or rather my kind-hearted wife and my daughter

Marie, adopted their boy, Friedrich (Fritz). He was treated so much as one of our own children that he hardly felt the loss of his parents at all. He is now a bookkeeper in a reputable wholesalers. He officially changed his name a short time ago to 'Hollitscher' and is an upright good boy.' Fritz helped his step siblings to emigrate and then went to Yugoslavia and in March 1944 he was deported from the island of Rab by the Ustaše and died in Auschwitz.

9   Richard Kann (1874-1944), Wilhelm's third cousin and best friend. He was one of the last of Wilhelm's friends to leave Vienna only getting to New York in March 1940 and joining his elder brother, Leo, there. His brother Leo was the father of Professor Robert A. Kann who taught at the faculty of the History Department at Rutgers University. Robert Kann devoted himself to the study and teaching of Austrian history, with a particular interest in examining forces of conflict, division, reconciliation, and integration. In 1976 he returned to Austria as visiting professor at the University of Vienna and was appointed Honorary Professor of Modern History just before his death in 1981.

10   Hanna Laufer (1867-1941) Wilhelm's sister, had been married to Sigmund Laufer. Wilhelm was constantly worried about her in the War and tried to get her and her daughter out on a domestic servant visa. She died of pneumonia in October 1941.

11   Moravian town of Ostrava (Mährisch Ostrau) in the Czech Republic; it had the third largest Jewish community in Czechoslovakia between the two world wars after Prague and Brno.

12   The failed attempt to assassinate Hitler was on 8 November 1939. Seven people were killed and many others were injured. The bomb was planted by Georg Elser in a purely individual act in opposition to the Nazi treatment of workers and preparations for war. He was working in an armaments factory, where he had access to explosives and he prepared and placed the device himself. The Nazis made an implausible claim that it was planned by British agents, but they never staged a trial and Elser was killed in Dachau on 16 April 1945. A. Grenville, 'Who was Georg Elser?' *AJR Journal*, vol. 9, No. 1, January 2009. https://ajr.org.uk/wp-content/uploads/2018/02/2009_january.pdf

13   Ida Kerner (née Wottitz) (1873-1951) was a cousin of Wilhelm's wife Marianne Tedesko. She was also the mother of Bettina Cohen who was in Alexandria, Egypt with Wilhelm's daughter Lisl. Ida was very musical and sang at Brahms' funeral and was very well read. She was a great companion during his time in Petts Wood.

14   Lili Bunzl (1885-1983) was the widow of Victor Bunzl, a brother of Martin Bunzl. She was also a Tedesko and a cousin of Wilhelm's wife Marianne in her own right.

15   Liesl Pelc (1912-1993) was the daughter of Lili Bunzl and mother of Hedi.

16   Martin Bunzl (1879-1952) was Wilhelm's benefactor and first cousin (double since a brother and sister married a brother and a sister) of his wife Marianne. Martin and Wilhelm were friends from their student days. He was the oldest of the cousins and the senior director of Bunzl and Biach. Husband of Grete (née Margarete Schönberg) Bunzl. Father of Max Alois Bunzl (who in 1939 was with his wife and two children in Buenos Aires), and Herbert Alois Bunzl. Brother of Robert Max Bunzl; Hugo Bunzl; Felix Bunzl; Georg Bunzl; Dr. Victor Bunzl; Alice Bunzl and Emil Bunzl.

17   This was probably the SS *Veendam* (II). This had had neutral lettering added to the ship's hull at the beginning of the war and on 17 September had saved part of the crew of the torpedoed aircraft carrier, H.M.S. *Courage*. When the Germans invaded the Netherlands on 10 May 1940, the ship was docked in Rotterdam and damaged. A year later it was seized and subsequently used as an accommodation ship for the German

navy. When Hamburg was liberated in May 1945, it was boarded by the British and, after the war, it was again used as a passenger ship from the Netherlands to New York. It was demolished in 1953. https://www.captainalbert.com/holland-line-ships-past-and-present/the-ss-veendam-of-1922/

18   Hans Schönberg's son. Hans was the chief operating and financial officer of Bunzl &Biach who was in Switzerland during the war. Friedl became the family lawyer for the Bunzl family, and according to Rudy Bunzl, was the dispenser of objective advice on handling numerous disagreements.

19   Gustav Schönberg (1880-1944) was the brother of Martin Bunzl's wife Grete and Hans Schönberg. He was interned with Wilhelm and was also clearly unwell during his time at Huyton and moved to a special diet hostel.

20   Carl Philipp Gottfried (or Gottlieb) von Clausewitz (1780–1831) was a Prussian general who was a seminal theorist of war. The Nazis used him as a source for their notions of total war, but his ideas were far more complex and nuanced than this.

21   Else Wottitz (née Weiss) was the widowed sister-in-law of Ida Kerner.

22   Hans Oppenheimer (1908-1985), husband of Wilhelm's daughter, Lisl. He was at this time working as a steel trader in Alexandria, Egypt. His sister and brother-in-law referred to on 30 August were in the Ardeche in Vichy France. His sister, Käte Haas, survived the war but his brother-in-law, Richard Haas, was taken to Drancy and then Auschwitz in 1942.

23   Dr Albert Hollitscher (1903-1943) was the son of Dr Marc Hollitscher, Wilhelm's brother. Albert left Vienna on 11 August 1939, his thirty-sixth birthday, to go to Milan, Italy, where he couldn't get a job. He could not get a visa for the USA and tried to get to Yugoslavia. Wilhelm describes him as gifted but one-sided and eccentric. In May 1940 he was imprisoned and sent to Germany. He was ultimately killed in a concentration camp.

24   Archibald Maule Ramsay was a Scottish Unionist MP with stridently antisemitic views. After involvement with a suspected spy at the American embassy, he was interned under Defence Regulation 18B. R. Griffiths, *Patriotism Perverted: Captain Ramsay, the Right Club, and British Anti-Semitism, 1939-1940* (London: Faber, 2011). Oswald Mosley, the founder of the British Union of Fascists (BUF), was interned under the same regulation.

25   J. Hadham, *Good God: A Study of his Character and Activities* (London: Penguin, 1940).

26   The fall of France caused panic, leading to a policy of wholesale internment, regardless of the earlier division into categories. After Italy declared war, any Italians resident in Britain were also interned, without any tribunal.

27   Dr Karl Weiss was Wilhelm's closest companion in Huyton. He had been an injured officer with commendation in WW1. He was the brother of Prof. Dr. Franz X. Weiss, 1885-1956, who was married to Dr. Cornelia [Nelly] Weiss (née Bunzl) who was the youngest daughter of Ludwig Lajos Bunzl 1857-1928, a brother of Max Bunzl (the father of all the children who ran Bunzl and Biach) and sister of Klara Tedesko (who was Marianne's mother). Nelly was therefore a first cousin of Marianne Tedesco, Wilhelm's wife. Karl and Franz's sister, Alice 1881-1979, was married to another of the Tedesko brothers, Victor and so was a sister-in-law of Marianne. Victor and Alice went to USA before the war. Franz and Nelly were part of the Petts Wood clan and he was an eminent academic in Austria where he edited Eugen von Böhm-Bawerk's work and was quoted by Hayek.

28 A medical doctor with a practice in Bromley, near Petts Wood. Wilhelm consulted him before internment about his thrombosis in his leg.

29 The grandstand at the racecourse was used for accommodation. Rachel Pistol, 'Enemy Alien and Refugee: Conflicting Identities in Great Britain during the Second World War', *University of Sussex Journal of Contemporary History* 16, 2015, p.38. https://www.sussex.ac.uk/webteam/gateway/file.php?name=pistol-enemy-alien.pdf&site=15

30 In fact, several hundred women and children were also arrested. Ibid.

31 Wilhelm met him at Kempton Park and they were moved together to Huyton. He was a director in Vienna of a Petroleum company. He left for the Isle of Man on 10 July. Wilhelm forwarded letters to him.

32 The camp was at an unfinished housing estate in Huyton, near Liverpool. Up to 5,000 German, Austrian and Italian civilians were held here and the government decided it would keep them in the camp long-term, rather than send them to the Isle of Man, Canada or Australia, as initially planned. The estate was chosen as it lay empty, but unfinished. Recent research highlights the scale of overcrowding, dismal healthcare and sanitation, poor diets and shelter, with internees sleeping in canvas tents in an area that became waterlogged and filthy, with no washing facilities. All the internees were released in mid-1941 as the threat of German invasion subsided. Tom Belger, 'Merseyside's wartime prison camp that you've never heard of', *Liverpool Echo*, 21 June 2015   http://www.liverpoolecho.co.uk/news/liverpool-news/merseysides-wartime-prison-camp-youve-9498601
However, conditions were far better than in the most notorious transit camp at Warth Mill, near Bury. Pistol, *Enemy Alien*, p.39.

33 Lekha Dodi is a sixteenth century Hebrew-language Jewish liturgical song recited on Friday at dusk, usually at sundown, in synagogues to welcome *Shabbat* prior to the evening services.

34 Air Marshall Italo Balbo was at the time governor-general and Italian commander-in-chief in the Fascist colony of Libya. He was seen as a rival to Mussolini and there was speculation that he had been murdered but experts have concluded this was an aerial accident. The reason Wilhelm calls his fellow cheering internees stupid is because Balbo opposed the alliance with Hitler 'Balbo greeted the news of Mussolini's decision to go to war at the Nazis' side with great sadness. He believed that the war would destroy Fascist Italy, his career, and his very life, and he would be proved right on all three counts.'   https://warfarehistorynetwork.com/2015/12/27/the-strange-death-of-air-marshal-italo-balbo/

35 As a French mandate, Syria sided with the Vichy French government after the fall of France in 1940. Maxime Weygand was a French military commander in the First and Second World Wars and Minister of Defence under Pétain in 1940.EugèneMittelhauser (7 August 1873-19 December 1949) was appointed in June 1940 to command the French forces in Syria. R.T. Thomas, *Britain and Vichy, The Dilemma of Anglo-French Relations, 1940-42* (London and Basingstoke: Macmillan, 1979), pp.53-87.

36 Viktor Bunzl (1917-2000) was the son of Emil Bunzl, one of Martin's brothers. He is the grandfather of Matti Bunzl who is the director of the Wien Museum in Vienna and the author of many books.

37 Professor Karl Weissenberg (1893-1976) was formerly from the University of Berlin and had worked in Southampton University since 1934. He was the Camp Father.

Though not a Nobel Prize winner, he was an outstanding physicist in the fields of rheology and crystallography. He was seriously ill and was eventually released, partly as a result of an appeal by Einstein. (Tony Kushner and Katharine Knox, *Refugees in an Age of Genocide: Global, National and Local Perspectives during the Twentieth Century* (London: Frank Cass, 1999), p.176.

38   Each house elected a 'house father' who reported to the 'street father' to make sure the general duties for the house were assigned to the men living there and to ensure their attendance at roll call. 'Street fathers' forwarded grievances and requests to the 'camp father' and ensured that the houses on their street were kept in order. This system was pioneered at Huyton and then also used on the Isle of Man. Pistol, *Enemy Alien*, p.42.

39   This refers to the British naval bombardment of the French navy at its base at Mers-el-Kébir and another attack at Dakar in order to ensure that the fleet was not taken over by the Germans. The raid on Mers-el-Kébir resulted in the deaths of 1,297 French servicemen and the severing of diplomatic relations between Vichy France and Britain. It remains controversial. Thomas, *Britain and Vichy*, pp.42-48.

40   Wilhelm met him in Salford and visited him and his wife. His wife was very musical and sang Schubert Lieder. They wrote regularly to each other. In June 1940, before they were interned, he notes that he has been employed as a research engineer at £5 a week in a factory. Fortunately, he survived internment.

41   Rudy Bunzl (1922-2016) was the younger son of Robert Bunzl, another brother of Martin. He worked in the US Filter Corporation, which became American Filtrona Company Georgia. He died in 2016 and before his death read our translation of Wilhelm's diary and corrected a couple of mistakes.

42   On 8 December 1938, Lord Baldwin gave a speech on the radio (which was also transmitted in the USA) to help raise funds for Jewish refugees. The appeal brought in over £500,000 in donations from over a million British people. Some of this money was used to lease the Palace Hotel on Bloomsbury Street, WC1, which was to become Bloomsbury House – the headquarters for around eleven refugee organisations working under the umbrella of the Central Office for Refugees.http:// www.kitchenercamp.co.uk/research/bloomsbury-house/

43   The reference was probably to Sir John Anderson, who was then the Home Secretary and Minister of Home Security.

44   The most controversial aspect of the whole internment policy was the transportation of just over 11,000 male internees to Canada and Australia. The original intention was to transport only those who posed the highest security risk, but because the government was unable to find enough 'dangerous' internees the quotas were completed arbitrarily. In the worst tragedy the *Arandora Star* was torpedoed on 2 July 1940, with the loss of 650 lives. The ship had included some 700 Italians and approximately 500 Germans. (Pistol, *Enemy Alien*, pp. 47-8). The round up mentioned in the diary was for the *Dunera* which departed on 10 July from Liverpool to Australia. Otto Lehmann-Russbueldt says: 'On the day appointed for departure the youngest of the internees were forced to depart at bayonet point. On that morning some of the designated deportees concealed themselves – I myself know of two young academics who did this.' (Jennifer Taylor (ed), *Civilian Internment in Britain During WW2: Huyton Camp. Eye-witness Accounts*, Southend-on-Sea, Anglo-German Family History Society Publications, p.49). There were many rumours about deportation and the Huyton

internees received the news of the *Arandora Star* on 5 July, which made them particularly scared.

45   '*Salzamt Eröffnet*' in the Viennese idiom means a fictitious bureaucratic institution without any function. There is a saying in Vienna that if you want something and it doesn't exist, you go to the salt office! Tent 999 clearly does not exist.

46   Ing. Leo Fischer (1890-1983) was the father of Hanna who married Gustl (Gustav George) Bunzl.

47   Gustl (Gustav George) Bunzl (1915-1981) was the eldest son of Hugo Bunzl. He built up the paper side of the Bunzl companies and led on Cigarette Components Ltd. He was already working in the Bunzl enterprise before the Second World War. He was briefly interned. He was married to Hanna Bunzl (née Fischer) whose father Ing Fischer was in the camp with Wilhelm.

48   Stephan Mittler shared the house at Huyton with Wilhelm and took on the fire warden role. He and Wilhelm clashed. He was clearly a very energetic man who tried to organise all the engineers and get them employed by the British Government rather than languishing in internment. But Wilhelm found him too bossy and without a sense of humour.

49   The French did bomb Gibraltar on 18 July in response to the attack on Mers-el-Kébir.

50   Southern Poland.

51   Wilhelm suffered from thrombosis in his legs.

52   Referred to on 28 June as a former lawyer of the British Embassy in Vienna.

53   This almost certainly referred to Eleanor Rathbone (1872-1946), who had set up the Parliamentary Committee on Refugees. She regularly criticized Osbert Peake, Undersecretary at the Home Office. For a full tribute to Rathbone's campaigning work, see Susan Cohen, 'Remembering Eleanor Rathbone', *The Association of Jewish Refugees*, April 2001. http://www.ajr.org.uk/index.cfm/section.journal/issue.Apr01/article=614. See also https://rememberingeleanorrathbone.wordpress.com/books-about-eleanor-rathbone/.

54   It is not clear who this is but on 5 July 1940 Michael Foot, Frank Owen and Peter Howard (under the pseudonym 'Cato') published the collaborative book, *Guilty Men* (London, Gollancz, 1940) expressing contempt for Neville Chamberlain's appeasement diplomacy.

55   The two main Dunkirk operations are not mentioned in the diary which is surprising. The first took place between 26 May and 4 June 1940. Operation Aerial was conducted 15–25 June 1940, Given that Wilhelm was only interned on the 27 June the lack of mention shows that these events were downplayed in the British press. He does later mention internees coming to the UK with the evacuated soldiers from Dunkirk and here he mentions 200 German planes attacking the convoys bringing back soldiers from France.

56   Philip Noel-Baker (1889-1982), Labour MP, was a prominent campaigner for internationalism, who would receive the Nobel Prize for Peace in 1959.

57   Hans Gottfurcht (1896-1982) was a German Jewish Social Democrat and union official, who created an underground union organisation after 1933. He was arrested by the Gestapo in July 1937, but the following year had managed to emigrate to London. From 1941, he chaired the British section of the exiled German trade unionists' organisation, edited its journal, and was on the party executive of the SPD in exile. http://www.gdw-berlin.de/nc/en/recess/biographies/biographie/view-bio/gottfurcht/

58   Wilhelm first read this book by John Hadham published by Penguin Books in 1940 before he was interned – see diary entry for 24 May 1940.

59   Wilhelm met Otto Hirschhorn when he was living in Salford in 1939. He referred to him as part of the youth refugee colony in Manchester; Otto was then 27 years old. They became friends, showing Wilhelm's ability to make good friends among young refugees, just as he later befriended Hugo Dachinger.

60   Hugo Bunzl (1883-1960) One of Martin's brothers and a key figure in the Bunzl and Biach companies. Hugo led on the Ortmann factory working with Emil, another brother. The company centerary booklet published in 1954 states that at all times the family attached 'much importance to human and social considerations and, particularly in Austria, welfare centres, playing fields and other social amenties have been provided'. The Hugo Bunzl Housing Estate was started in 1923 and there was a kindergarten and workers' club in Ortmann. Hugo was particularly responsible for the success of the companies through the development of Tissue Papers Ltd (TPL which in 1951 became Bunzl Pulp and Paper Limited [BPP]) and its subsidiary Cigarette Components Ltd (CC later called Filtrona), which produced cigarette filters.

61   Wilhelm refers in his Epilogue to Fascists at high levels of government who try to sabotage those who want to oppose Hitler. He mentions his knowledge of what happened to Hans Gottfurcht in this context. He is therefore not referring here only to interrogations by the Gestapo in Germany but also to their sympathisers in the UK. This history is particularly revealed in the treatment of Dora Fabian. Charmian Brinson and Richard Dove, *A Matter of Intelligence: MI5 and the surveillance of anti-Nazi refugees, 1933-50* (Oxford, Oxford University Press, 2016) and Charmian Brinson, *The Strange Case of Dora Fabian and Mathilde Wurm : a study of German political exiles in London during the 1930s* (Berne: Peter Lang, 1996).

62   This is his first meeting with Hugo Dachinger

63   Dr. jur. Theodor Erlanger (1880-1956); his license to practice at the Superior District Court and District Courts Munich I and II was withdrawn (with that of 91 others) under Nazi policies to exclude and persecute Jewish lawyers. Susanne Rieger, 'The Exclusion of Jewish Lawyers in Bavaria in December 1938' (2003) http://www.rijo.homepage.t-online.de/pdf/EN_BY_JU_anwalt02.pdf

64   Each internee had an account in which the money he had brought with him was deposited. Each internee was permitted to receive ten shillings per week from outside the camp, but remittances had to be sent to the Commandant's office (see Taylor, *Civilian Internment in Britain during WW2*, p.94).

65   Harry was a nephew of Gustav Hollitscher, the husband of Wilhelm's sister, Ida. He was therefore not a blood relative. He was in USA. He liaised with a solicitor called Weinberger whom Wilhelm had entrusted with some money for his niece Stella. Wilhelm accused Weinberger of stealing all Stella's money.

66   Lt Colonel Slatter was appointed Commandant on 15 July replacing the previous Commandant who had feared a riot and was unwilling or unable to mitigate the poor conditions in the camp. He had formerly held responsibility for the camps on the Isle of Man, and he came to Huyton with a reformist agenda so conditions gradually improved. J. Taylor (ed.), 2012 *Civilian Internment in Britain During WW": Huyton Camp Eye-Witness Accounts* (Southend-on-Sea: Anglo-German Family History Society Publications, 2012), p.14.

67   Hans was the brother of Edith Popper (1910-2002) who was the best friend of Wilhelm's daughter, Lisl. Both Hans and Edith went to the USA and Edith married (Edith Hacker) and became a doctor.

68   He was a relation of Wilhelm's sister Hanna's husband. He came to London and left with his wife in May 1940 for the USA. He gave a reference for Wilhelm's son Hansl to help him find employment in the USA.

69   George Bell was the Bishop of Chichester and Rabbi Dr Solomon Schonfeld was the son-in-law of the Chief Rabbi. They visited the camp on the 18 July. Rabbi Schonfeld personally rescued many thousands of Jews from Nazi forces in Central and Eastern Europe during the years 1938-1948 and facilitated the Kindertransport. D. Taylor, *Solomon Schonfeld: A Purpose in Life* (London: Vallentine Mitchell, 2009).

70   The Bishop of Chichester reported on his visits to Huyton and the Isle of Man in the House of Lords on 6 August 1940, urging the need to distinguish between true 'enemy aliens' and the majority of internees who were refugees and should be released. http://hansard.millbanksystems.com/lords/1940/aug/06/internment-of-aliens

71   This may be the blue costume that he wore for the portrait by Dachinger.

72   Eleanor Rathbone (MP representing the Universities) visited the camp on 20 July 1940, with H. Graham White (MP for Birkenhead East), a member of her all-party Parliamentary Committee. S.Cohen, *Rescue the Perishing: Eleanor Rathbone and the Refugees* (London: Vallentine Mitchell, 2010).

73   Anderson made a statement on 23 July 1940. This referred to some exemptions from the general policy and particularly to persons who had been interned who should have been exempted on grounds of ill-health or infirmity. http://hansard. millbanksystems.com/commons/1940/jul/23/internees-government-proposalsagreed

74   Probably an engineering journal published in Berlin.

75   Many of the 'notices' are in-jokes, like the suggestion that women hairdressers are sought when the camp was only for men.

76   Yiddish: a person, especially a man, who is regarded as pitifully ineffectual, or submissive.

77   The camp only opened on 17 May. Taylor, *Civilian Internment in Britain during WW2*, p.78.

78   'In addition to the material hardship, which camp life entailed, internees faced the harsher trial of isolation occasioned by the abrupt severance of contact with their families. Internees were only permitted to write two letters a week' and these were limited to twenty four lines. The censorship of mail also delayed the post. The Camp Commandant visited the Chief Censor at Liverpool on the 22 July rather than going to London. Taylor, *Civilian Internment in Britain during WW2*, pp.93-94.

79   Christian Johann Heinrich Heine (1797-1856) was a German Jewish poet, writer, literary critic and radical. In 1825 he converted to Protestantism, seeing his conversion as 'the ticket of admission into European culture'. Quoted by J. Sammons, *Heinrich Heine: A Modern Biography* (Princeton: Princeton University Press, 1980), p. 109, who also doubts whether Heine's motives were so cynical as this passage implies. Heine lived in Paris from 1831. His books were burned by the Nazis who hated his work.

80   This is probably Alfred Oppenheim, a friend of Richard Kann who left Vienna very late in 1940 with Richard to go to New York.

81   Franz Tedesko (1891-1952) was Marianne Hollitscher's brother. He and his wife Grete Tedesko and son Peter Tedesko lived in London at this time. Franz has a major operation which was why he was not interned.

82   Onkel Gustl Bunzl (1868-1941) was a friend of Wilhelm and was suffering from stomach cancer. He was the only survivor of 4 children produced by Moritz Bunzl (the grandfather of Martin and his brothers and Marianne Hollitscher and her Tedesco brothers) and his second wife Laura. He was therefore a half-brother of Klara and Max Bunzl. Rudy Bunzl said: 'I remember him. He was an insurance agent and somewhat peculiar. He is not be confused with whom our generation called Gustl or GG (Gustav George), Hugo's oldest son and future head of Bunzl plc.'

83   Karl Tedesko (1874-1945) was Marianne's brother living during the war in Lucerne, Switzerland. He facilitated letters between family members and tried very hard in the early period of the war to get his sister out of Vienna, unfortunately unsuccessfully.

84   Books and cigarettes could only be sent via a commercial outlet. Taylor, *Civilian Internment in Britain during WW2*, p.100. Cigarettes were sold in the canteen. Ibid., p.89.

85   Leopolstadt was the Jewish quarter of Vienna in the inter-war period. In Hungarian a *schliferl* is a little thief who avoids authority. http://mnytud.arts.klte.hu/szleng/ regi/bptolvny.htm

86   A Sunday newspaper owned by the Co-operative Press and linked to the Co-operative Party.

87   H G Wells in *Reynolds News* began a series of articles attributing the policy of general internment to treachery. Miriam Kochen, *Britain's Internees in the Second World War* (London and Basingstoke: Macmillan Press, 1983), p.120.

88   Wells apparently accused the Home Office of being run by Nazi sympathisers. M.Ritchie, 'Exile, Internment and Deportation' in R. Dove (ed.) *"Totally Un-English"? Britain's Internment of 'Enemy Aliens' in Two World Wars* (Amsterdam and New York: Rodopi BV, 2005), p.199.

89   This refers to a meeting of the Pan American Conference in Havana (27-30 July) where it was decided to establish trusteeships over European colonies in the Western Hemisphere, whose mother countries had been overrun by the Germans. This policy applied to Dutch and French colonies in the Caribbean, in South America, and off the Canadian coast. The stated goal was for the American states as a whole to prevent Fascist infiltration into the Western Hemisphere through these colonies. U.S. Congress, *Global Defense: U.S. Military Commitments Abroad* (US: Washington, DC: Congressional Quarterly Service, 1969), p.10.

90   A small Jewish town or village before the Second World War, in Eastern Europe.

91   Wilhelm's brother, Dr Jacob Hans Hollitscher,(referred to as Hans or Hanspoldi, 1875-1947), was married to Poldi. At this time they were in poverty in Zurich. Hans was born Jacob Hans but called Hans after his oldest brother who died when he was two. He was almost forty when he graduated in 1914 with Doctorates in both Law and Philosophy and he then became a lawyer, but he also had some experience in banking. One consistent aspect in his adult life seems to have been a concern with the need to ensure full employment and welfare expenditure, and a preoccupation with the role of banking and money in this context. He was very involved in the *Wörgl* Experiment, to generate full employment through public expenditure. His major work was *Katastrophenwirtschaft. Geburt und Ende Österreichs 1918 bis 1938* (Disaster Management: Birth and the End of Austria, 1918-39). He went to Zurich in 1938 and subsequently became both a British and American spy. See C. Turner, *The CASSIA Spy Ring in World War II: A History of the OSS's Maier-Messner Group* (Jefferson, North Carolina: MacFarland, 2017).

92 This was probably Hans Ludwig Hamburger (1889-1956). He arrived in Britain and was a lecturer at the University of Southampton from 1941-56. No evidence has been found that he was at Huyton, but it seems very likely.

93 The notice opening the Viennese café read: 'The Economics Centre announces that a Camp Café will be opened today at 3:00pm at 50 Bruton Rd. The Café will be run by internees for internees. All profits will go exclusively to the Welfare Fund. Popular prices. Please help us in providing a comfortable place for you and assisting our comrades in need.' See Taylor, *Civilian Internment in Britain during WW2*, p91.

94 Oskar Kraus (1872 –1942) was a Czech philosopher and jurist who converted to Protestantism. He wrote about Albert Schweitzer in the 1920s in German and his book about him was published in English as *Albert Schweitzer: His Work and his Philosophy*, (London: Adam and Charles Black, 1944). The reference is to the Oxford Group, founded by the American Christian missionary, Dr Frank Buchman, who believed that the root of all problems was fear and selfishness. It was originally called 'A First Century Christian Fellowship' when established in 1921 and became known as the 'Oxford Group' by 1931. After 1938 it became known as 'Moral re-armament'.

95 Julius Streicher was the founder and publisher of *Der Stürmer*, a central element in Nazi anti-semitic propaganda. Despite his special relationship with Hitler, after 1938 Streicher's position began to unravel. He was accused of corruption, adultery and spreading untrue stories about Göring. In February 1940 he was stripped of his party offices and withdrew from the public eye, although he was permitted to continue publishing *Der Stürmer*. The rumour about his death was false. He was sentenced to death at Nuremberg on 1 October 1946. 'Julius Streicher, The Beast of Franconia', Holocaust Education and Archive Research Team. http://www.holocaustresearch project.org/holoprelude/streicher.html

96 Professor Arthur Liebert (Levy) (1878-1946) was a Neo-Kantian philosopher. He converted to Protestantism in 1905 and changed his name from Levy to Liebert. He came to England in 1939 and became head of the Free German University, which opened in July 1942.

97 Anny Winiewicz (1905-1942) was the daughter of Wilhelm's brother Marc Hollitscher. She married Karl Winiewicz. He was interned in Provinz, Silesia in 1939. Wilhelm says 'Anni married to a talented but passive chap and she herself is incapable to forge her own existence'. She did however manage to get to Vichy France but both Karl and Anni were murdered in Oświęcim in Poland in 1942. Karl's children, her step children, were only one quarter Jewish and survived the war in Vienna.

98 Wilhelm translates this as 'very enjoyable'.

99 Bad Goisern am Hallstättersee is a market town in the Austrian state of Upper Austria.

100 Yiddish for the Sabbath.

101 Marianne Hollitscher (née Tedesko, 1885-1941) was the fifth child of six Tedesco children and the only girl. She married Wilhelm in May 1908 and had two children, Lisl and Hansl. But by 1939 the couple were estranged and she decided not to go with him to the UK. She was deported from Vienna and shot on arrival in Kaunas County, Lithuania on 29 November 1941 aged 56.

102 Robert Ensor, *England 1870-1914* (Oxford: Oxford University Press, 1936).

103 Lord Lytton, 2nd Earl of Lytton (9 August 1876 – 25 October 1947), was a British politician and colonial administrator. He served as Governor of Bengal between 1922 and 1927 and was briefly Acting Viceroy of India in 1926. Lytton may be best known

for his chairmanship of the Lytton Commission, which was sent by the League of Nations on a fact-finding mission to determine who was to blame in the 1931 war between Japan and China. It was hoped that the report would defuse the hostilities between Japan and China and would thus help maintain peace and stability in the Far East. The commission's Lytton Report, officially issued on 1 October 1932, caused Japan to withdraw from the League of Nations. In August 1940 he was appointed chair of the Advisory Council on aliens, which was attached to the Foreign Office, which was chiefly concerned with the welfare of internees. There was a separate Advisory Committee under the War Office whose role was to: 'To keep under review the application of the principles laid down in regard to the internment of enemy aliens'. http://hansard.millbanksystems.com/lords/1940/aug/15/internment-of-aliens

104 The Nansen passports were issued in 1922, following an international agreement at the Intergovernmental Conference on Identity Certificates for Russian Refugees convened by Fridtjof Nansen, the High Commissioner for Refugees for the League of Nations.

105 The crash, on 13 August, was in fact near Canberra. The deaths of the three cabinet ministers weakened the United Australia government of Robert Menzies, contributing to its fall the next year. A. Tink, *Air Disaster Canberra: The Plane Crash that Destroyed a Government* (Sydney: UNSW Press, 2013).

106 Robert Bunzl (1882-1977) was another of Martin's brothers. He founded the London company Bunzl & Biach (British) Ltd in 1936. In 1940 the brothers agreed that Robert and his family should move to USA and establish a family business there as 'insurance' in case Hitler were to overrun England. Robert founded the Textile and Paper Supply Corporation in Atlanta.

107 The chances of a bomb falling were much greater than this, as Liverpool was only 4 miles away and the Liverpool docks were 7 miles away. Wilhelm mentions a bomb falling near the football pitch on 29 August. As Wilhelm notes earlier they were poorly prepared. There were no air raid shelters and permission to dig these, using internee labour, had been refused. Medical support was highly dependent on the refugees themselves. Taylor, *Civilian Internment in Britain during WW2*, p.106-111

108 In conventional accounts of the Battle of Britain, there was an air war from 10 July until 31 October, but after 7 September, the Nazis became aware that Germany was failing to win the air fight and began the relentless bombing of British cities in the Blitz. Historians have now shown that the reality was far more complex than these conventional accounts, which have included much myth and propaganda. See R. Overy, Battle of Britain and the Blitz' *Oxford Bibliographies* (last reviewed April 2017). https://www.oxfordbibliographies.com/view/document/obo-9780199791279/obo-9780199791279-0158.xml .

109 Julius Oppenheimer (1871-1931) was Hans Oppenheimer's uncle who founded the steel company in Egypt where Hans worked from 1929-1949.

110 Josef Popper-Lynkeus (1838-1931) was the uncle of Karl Popper. He would have appealed to Wilhelm as he was an engineer and an inventor who also wrote books on social philosophy. Like Wilhelm he was therefore grounded in looking for practical ways of improving human life. According to Popper-Lynkeus, the right to exist is the primary and natural right of any human being and the state has a duty to provide the necessities of life and does not have the right to condemn anyone to death without the person's consent. His 'general nutritional obligation' or 'the obligation to provide goods

of primary necessity' was formulated in three major works: *The Right to Live and the Duty to Die* (1878); *The Individual and the Evaluation of Human Existence;* and finally *General nutritional obligation as a solution to the social question* (1912). He argued that every citizen should have the right to a minimum subsistence level of goods.

111 Statement in the House of Commons, 22 August 1940.

112 Yiddish word used here to mean awkwardness or shame – Dr F. is seen as a little senile which is rather embarrassing to Wilhelm.

113 Trotsky was assassinated in Mexico by Ramón Mercader on 20 August, but died the next day. Mercader was a Spanish Communist and a Soviet agent and served 20 years in prison. Stalin awarded him an Order of Lenin and he was given the title, 'Hero of the Soviet Union' after his release from prison in 1961.

114 Gerti Hollitscher (1906-1987) was the only one of Wilhelm's brother Marc's children to survive the war. She trained as a doctor and ultimately got a doctor's job in the British Army sometime after she came to England.

115 Hitler had already annexed large areas of western Poland in October 1939, with a population of approximately ten million. The area to which the diary refers were the four districts that were placed under the so-called General Government under the control of the Nazi, Hans Frank, who oversaw the segregation of the Jews into ghettos, was found guilty of war crimes against humanity at the Nuremburg trials and subsequently executed. Philippe Sands, *East West Street: On the origins of genocide and crimes against humanity* (London: Weidenfeld and Nicolson, 2016).

116 Kremers is making an English pun. 'Erez Israel' literally translates as 'Land of Israel(s)'and is the traditional Hebrew name for the country.

117 Herbert Alois Bunzl (1910-1989) was Martin Bunzl's son who married Trude Bunzl (1924-2013) and settled in Chislehurst, next to Petts Wood, and had seven children. Martin together with Herbert and Trude looked after my family when we arrived in England in 1949.

118 See 27 November 1939.

119 None of these three were, in fact, members of the government, but all were committed opponents of Fascism. H.G. Wells, the writer, published a pamphlet, *The New World Order,* in January 1940 (London: Secker and Warburg, 1940), arguing for unity between the nations of the world in order to bring peace and end war, with a legal system to protect human rights. It is now available as an ebook through Project Gutenberg, Australia, on http://gutenberg.net.au/ebooks04/0400671h.html. Josiah Wedgwood was a Labour MP, who had been an early critic of Hitler, who had argued for changes in the law so as to allow Germans fleeing from Fascism to come to Britain and he chaired the German Refugee Hospitality Committee. Lord Rusholme was acting President of the International Co-operative Alliance from 1940-46 (and subsequently President in his own right from 1946-48) and was a thorough-going internationalist.

120 This was in the Second Vienna Award of 30 August 1940, under which Nazi Germany and Fascist Italy reassigned the territory of Northern Transylvania from Romania to Hungary, thereby reversing the Treaty of Trianon of 1920.

Index

Note: Page numbers followed by 'n' refer to notes; **Bold** page numbers refer to photographs